Southern Living

FEEL GOOD FOOD

Oxmoor House

ISBN-13: 978-0-8487-3691-0
ISBN-10: 0-8487-3691-5
Library of Congress Control Number: 2012949306

Printed in the United States of America
First Printing 2013

Oxmoor House
Editorial Director: Leah McLaughlin
Creative Director: Felicity Keane
Senior Brand Manager: Daniel Fagan
Senior Editor: Rebecca Brennan
Managing Editor: Rebecca Benton

Southern Living Feel Good Food
Editor: Susan Hernandez Ray
Art Director: Claire Cormany
Project Editor: Sarah H. Doss
Senior Designer: Melissa Clark
Director, Test Kitchen: Elizabeth Tyler Austin
Assistant Directors, Test Kitchen: Julie Christopher, Julie Gunter
Recipe Developers and Testers: Wendy Ball, R.D.;
    Victoria E. Cox; Tamara Goldis; Stefanie Maloney;
    Callie Nash; Karen Rankin; Leah Van Deren
Recipe Editor: Alyson Moreland Haynes
Food Stylists: Margaret Monroe Dickey,
    Catherine Crowell Steele
Photography Director: Jim Bathie
Senior Photographer: Helene Dujardin
Senior Photo Stylist: Kay E. Clarke
Photo Stylist: Mindi Shapiro Levine
Assistant Photo Stylist: Mary Louise Menendez
Senior Production Manager: Greg A. Amason

***Southern Living*®**
Editor: M. Lindsay Bierman
Creative Director: Robert Perino
Managing Editor: Candace Higginbotham
Art Director: Chris Hoke
Executive Editors: Rachel Hardage Barrett, Hunter Lewis,
    Jessica S. Thuston
Food Director: Shannon Sliter Satterwhite
Test Kitchen Director: Rebecca Kracke Gordon
Senior Writer: Donna Florio
Senior Food Editor: Mary Allen Perry
Recipe Editor: JoAnn Weatherly
Assistant Recipe Editor: Ashley Arthur
Test Kitchen Specialist/Food Styling: Vanessa McNeil Rocchio
Test Kitchen Professionals: Norman King, Pam Lolley,
    Angela Sellers
Senior Photographers: Ralph Lee Anderson, Gary Clark,
    Art Meripol
Photographers: Robbie Caponetto, Laurey W. Glenn
Photo Research Coordinator: Ginny P. Allen
Senior Photo Stylist: Buffy Hargett
Editorial Assistant: Pat York
Contributing Editor: Virginia Willis

Contributors
Writer: Valerie Fraser Luesse
Recipe Developers and Testers: Erica Hopper, Tonya Johnson,
    Kyra Moncrief, Kathleen Royal Phillips
Copy Editors: Donna Baldone, Norma Butterworth-McKittrick
Proofreader: Adrienne Davis
Indexer: Mary Ann Laurens
Interns: Morgan Bolling, Susan Kemp, Alicia Lavender, Sara Lyon,
    Staley McIlwain, Emily Robinson, Maria Sanders, Katie Strasser
Food Stylists: Ana Kelly, Marian Cooper Cairns
Photographers: Beau Gustafson, Becky Stayner
Photo Stylists: Anna Pollock, Leslie Simpson, Caitlin Van Horn

Time Home Entertainment Inc.
Publisher: Jim Childs
VP, Strategy & Business Development: Steven Sandonato
Executive Director, Marketing Services: Carol Pittard
Executive Director, Retail & Special Sales: Tom Mifsud
Director, Bookazine Development & Marketing: Laura Adam
Executive Publishing Director: Joy Butts
Associate Publishing Director: Megan Pearlman
Finance Director: Glenn Buonocore
Associate General Counsel: Helen Wan

CONTENTS

FOREWORD

Fried chicken landed me a job at *Southern Living,* or at least brought me luck during my interview. John Floyd, who was the magazine's longtime editor-in-chief, gave me two choices for our lunch meeting—white-tablecloth fare at a gourmet restaurant or fried chicken at Birmingham's legendary Irondale Cafe. A few days later, the two of us were in line at the Irondale, holding out our cafeteria trays for servings of that crispy, golden Southern wonder. The magazine would become my home away from home for many happy years, and I still think of John whenever I have a particularly fine piece of chicken.

That's what *Feel Good Food* is all about—the wonderful associations we have with our favorite comfort foods, the memories they evoke, and the emotions they stir. I can have a slice of pound cake and feel instantly loved because it reminds me of my Aunt Vivian, who often brought one when she came to visit. Homemade spicy mustard reminds me of laughter in the kitchen with my culinary-challenged paternal grandmother. That mustard was the only recipe she ever flawlessly executed! Coconut cake equals Mama's Christmas table. Peach cobbler? The Fourth of July, when Aunt Joyce's 9x13 baking dish would be bubbling over with it. My cousin Mary's amazing sweet tea? Just one sip, even in the dead of

winter, conjures the memory of a beautiful summer day, with the whole family gathered together for a barbecue. (I'll give her a call and see if she's home so we can all swing by for a glass.)

Whether you're in the mood to rejuvenate or celebrate, whether you crave something warm and filling or "something sweet to finish off on," as my maternal grandmother used to say, you'll find it here. This wonderful collection of more than 200 recipes—each one carefully chosen by the *Southern Living* Food Editors—includes all the classics you'll want to pass along and pass down, but with fresh twists for modern families.

Because I love talking about great food as much as they love creating it, my friends at *Southern Living* invited me to share stories about some of my favorites. Think of these little reminiscences as the garnish for the recipes. And really—would you carry a banana pudding to the fellowship hall without adding that little ring of vanilla wafers around the top for decoration? Not if Mama has anything to do with it.

So sit a spell, and enjoy! *(Southern translation: Y'all c'mon to the table while everything's hot!)*

Valerie Fraser Luesse

REJUVENATED

breakfast

spicy ham-and-eggs Benedict with chive biscuits (pictured on opposite page)

makes: 4 servings   hands-on time: 30 min.   total time: 55 min.

4   frozen biscuits
2   Tbsp. butter, melted
3   Tbsp. chopped fresh chives, divided
1   (0.9-oz.) envelope hollandaise sauce mix
1   cup milk
1   Tbsp. lemon juice
¾   cup chopped lean ham
¼   to ½ tsp. ground red pepper
½   tsp. white vinegar
4   large eggs
2   cups loosely packed arugula
1   small avocado, sliced
Pepper to taste

1. Bake biscuits according to package directions. Combine melted butter and 1 Tbsp. chives; split biscuits, and brush with butter mixture. Preheat oven to 375°. Place biscuits, buttered sides up, on a baking sheet, and bake at 375° for 5 minutes or until toasted.

2. Prepare hollandaise sauce mix according to package directions, using 1 cup milk and 1 Tbsp. lemon juice and omitting butter.

3. Cook ham, stirring occasionally, in a medium-size nonstick skillet over medium heat 3 to 4 minutes or until browned. Stir ham and ground red pepper into hollandaise sauce; keep warm.

4. Add water to depth of 2 inches in a large saucepan. Bring to a boil; reduce heat, and maintain at a light simmer. Add ½ tsp. white vinegar. Break eggs, and slip into water, 1 at a time, as close as possible to surface of water. Simmer 3 to 5 minutes or to desired degree of doneness. Remove with a slotted spoon. Trim edges, if desired.

5. Place bottom biscuit halves, buttered sides up, on each of 4 individual serving plates. Top with arugula, avocado, and poached eggs. Spoon hollandaise sauce evenly on top of each egg. Sprinkle with remaining 2 Tbsp. chives and pepper to taste. Top with remaining biscuit halves, and serve immediately.

note: We tested with White Lily Southern Style Biscuits.

maple-pecan bacon

makes: 8 servings   hands-on time: 10 min.   total time: 40 min.

8   thick bacon slices
¼   cup maple syrup
1½ cups finely chopped pecans

1. Preheat oven to 400°. Place a lightly greased wire rack in an aluminum foil-lined 15- x 10-inch jelly-roll pan. Dip bacon slices in syrup, allowing excess to drip off; press pecans onto both sides of bacon. Arrange bacon slices in a single layer on rack. Bake at 400° for 20 minutes; turn bacon slices, and bake 5 to 10 more minutes or until browned and crisp. Remove from oven, and let stand 5 minutes.

Y'ALL ENJOY

Summer Brunch

8 servings

Tomato-Herb Mini Frittatas

Fruit Salad with Yogurt *(page 19)*

Gouda Grits *(page 19)*

Biscuits

Sparkling Ginger-Orange Cocktails *(page 40)*

tomato-herb mini frittatas

(pictured on opposite page, top left)

makes: 8 servings   hands-on time: 15 min.   total time: 30 min.

12 large eggs
1   cup half-and-half
½   tsp. salt
¼   tsp. freshly ground pepper
2   Tbsp. chopped fresh chives
1   Tbsp. chopped fresh parsley
1   tsp. chopped fresh oregano
1   pt. grape tomatoes, halved
1½ cups (6 oz.) shredded Italian three-cheese blend

1. Preheat oven to 450°. Process first 4 ingredients in a blender until blended. Stir together chives and next 2 ingredients in a small bowl. Place 8 lightly greased 4-inch (6-oz.) ramekins on 2 baking sheets; layer tomatoes, 1 cup cheese, and chive mixture in ramekins. Pour egg mixture over top, and sprinkle with remaining ½ cup cheese.

2. Bake at 450° for 7 minutes, placing 1 baking sheet on middle oven rack and other on lower oven rack. Switch baking sheets, and bake 7 to 8 more minutes or until set. Remove top baking sheet from oven; transfer bottom sheet to middle rack, and bake 1 to 2 more minutes or until lightly browned.

Try This Twist!

tomato-herb frittata: Prepare recipe as directed, substituting a lightly greased 13- x 9-inch baking dish for ramekins and increasing bake time to 18 to 20 minutes or until set.

note: Mixture will rise about 1 inch above rim of baking dish.
hands-on time: 10 min.; total time: 30 min.

okra-shrimp beignets

We took two Lowcountry favorites, okra and shrimp, and fried them into fritters that have the crispy and airy qualities of a good beignet, hence the name.

makes: about 30
hands-on time: 27 min.
total time: 47 min., including salsa and sour cream

Peanut oil
2   cups sliced fresh okra
½   green bell pepper, diced
½   medium onion, diced
1   large egg
½   cup all-purpose flour
¼   cup heavy cream
1   jalapeño pepper, finely chopped
¾   tsp. salt
¼   tsp. freshly ground pepper
¼   lb. unpeeled, medium-size raw shrimp, peeled and coarsely chopped
Fresh Tomato Salsa
Cilantro Sour Cream

1. Pour oil to depth of 3 inches into a Dutch oven; heat to 350°.

2. Stir together okra and next 8 ingredients in a large bowl until well blended; stir in shrimp.

3. Drop batter by rounded tablespoonfuls into hot oil, and fry, in batches, 2 to 3 minutes on each side or until golden brown. Drain on a wire rack over paper towels. Serve with Fresh Tomato Salsa and Cilantro Sour Cream.

Fresh Tomato Salsa: Stir together 4 large plum tomatoes, seeded and chopped (about 2 cups); ¼ cup chopped fresh cilantro; 1 jalapeño pepper, seeded and finely diced; 3 Tbsp. finely diced red onion; 2½ Tbsp. fresh lime juice; 1 Tbsp. extra virgin olive oil; and salt and pepper to taste. Garnish with cilantro, if desired.

Cilantro Sour Cream: Stir together 1 (8-oz.) container sour cream, ¼ cup chopped fresh cilantro, 1 tsp. lime zest, 1 tsp. fresh lime juice, and salt and pepper to taste.

Charleston Firsts

There are cities, and then there are *dream* cities. Charleston, that legendary jewel by the sea, never fails to fascinate, whether you're a history buff, a serious shopper, or a lover of fine food and romantic Southern gardens. Since I fancy myself in the "all of the above" camp, you can imagine how excited I was about my first trip there. I was traveling with my friend Susan, a bona fide "foodie," who took me restaurant-hopping. We'd have an appetizer here, an entrée there, here a dessert, there a beverage . . . Under her tutelage, I explored the joys of shrimp and grits and she-crab soup. That might've been a mistake because I will forever compare any versions of those iconic dishes with "the way they make them in Charleston." We had creamy bisques and rich coffees and collard greens that had been slow-cooking since the Roosevelt administration. Later, another friend and Charleston native told me about *Charleston Receipts,* the oldest Junior League cookbook in print. Excited by the possibility of duplicating those unforgettable flavors from my first visit, I bought a copy, thinking I would start with something simple, like a beverage recipe. Here's the first line I read: *Go to Old Market in June and get a quart of wild cherries . . .* On second thought, maybe I'll just e-mail Susan to see when she can meet me on King Street.

VFL

shrimp and grits

makes: 6 servings
hands-on time: 25 min.   total time: 30 min.

½ tsp. salt
1 cup uncooked quick-
  cooking grits
½ cup freshly grated
  Parmesan cheese

½ tsp. freshly ground
  pepper

1. Bring ½ tsp. salt and 4 cups water to a boil in a medium saucepan; gradually whisk in grits. Cook over medium heat, stirring occasionally, 8 minutes or until thickened. Whisk in cheese and pepper. Keep warm.

creamy shrimp sauce

1 lb. unpeeled, medium-
  size raw shrimp
¼ tsp. freshly ground
  pepper
⅛ tsp. salt
Vegetable cooking spray
1 Tbsp. olive oil
1 Tbsp. all-purpose flour
1¼ cups low-sodium
  fat-free chicken broth

½ cup chopped green
  onions
2 garlic cloves, minced
1 Tbsp. fresh lemon juice
¼ tsp. salt
¼ tsp. hot sauce
2 cups firmly packed fresh
  baby spinach

1. Peel shrimp; devein, if desired. Sprinkle shrimp with pepper and ⅛ tsp. salt. Cook in a large nonstick skillet coated with cooking spray over medium-high heat 1 to 2 minutes on each side or just until shrimp turn pink. Remove from skillet.

2. Reduce heat to medium. Add oil; heat 30 seconds. Whisk in flour; cook 30 seconds to 1 minute. Whisk in broth and next 5 ingredients; cook 2 to 3 minutes or until thickened. Stir in shrimp and spinach; cook 1 minute or until spinach is slightly wilted. Serve immediately over grits.

breakfast

17

gouda grits (pictured on opposite page)

makes: 8 servings
hands-on time: 10 min.   total time: 30 min.

4 cups chicken broth	½ cup buttermilk
1 cup whipping cream	¼ cup butter
1 tsp. salt	2 tsp. hot sauce
¼ tsp. freshly ground pepper	Garnish: shredded
2 cups uncooked quick-cooking grits	Gouda cheese, chopped green onions,
2 cups (8 oz.) shredded Gouda cheese	black pepper

1. Bring first 4 ingredients and 4 cups water to a boil in a Dutch oven over high heat; whisk in grits, reduce heat to medium-low, and simmer, stirring occasionally, 15 minutes or until thickened. Remove from heat, and stir in Gouda and next 3 ingredients. Garnish, if desired.

fruit salad with yogurt

The fruit can be made up to 1 day ahead of time. Simply toss the fruit together in a serving bowl, cover it, and refrigerate.

makes: 8 servings
hands-on time: 30 min.   total time: 30 min.

4 cups fresh pineapple chunks	2 (4-oz.) containers fresh raspberries
1 qt. strawberries, hulled and sliced in half	2 cups Greek yogurt
3 cups seedless green grapes	1 Tbsp. dark brown sugar
2 mangoes, peeled and sliced	1 Tbsp. honey

1. Toss together first 5 ingredients in a large serving bowl. Spoon yogurt into a separate serving bowl; sprinkle yogurt with sugar, and drizzle with honey. Serve fruit with yogurt mixture.

RASPBERRIES

Whether piled atop whipped cream on a buttery pound cake or crowning drizzled chocolate on a cheesecake, there's just something about these little red berries that adds an elegance to dishes. Intensely flavored, raspberries are composed of many connecting sections of fruit, each with its own seed, surrounding a central core. Be sure to take advantage of this fruit's best availability, which typically runs May to November.

When purchasing fresh raspberries at the grocery store, pick the ones that are plump and tender, but not mushy. They're sold in clear packaging, so make sure to check all sides for signs of poor quality. When you get them home, store them in an airtight container in the refrigerator 2 to 3 days.

Y'ALL ENJOY

Build Your Own Biscuit Buffet

8 servings

Angel Biscuits

Cornbread Biscuits with Crispy Chicken Cutlets *(page 24)*

Flavorful Preserves *(page 23)*

Up-a-Notch Sausage and Gravy *(page 23)*

---

angel biscuits (pictured on opposite page, top left)

Adding yeast guarantees fluffy biscuits every time.

makes: about 2 dozen   hands-on time: 20 min.   total time: 32 min.

1 (¼-oz.) envelope active dry yeast
¼ cup warm water (105° to 115°)
5 cups all-purpose flour
2 Tbsp. sugar
1 Tbsp. baking powder
1 tsp. baking soda
1 tsp. salt
½ cup shortening, cut into pieces
½ cup cold butter, cut into pieces
1½ cups buttermilk

1. Preheat oven to 400°. Combine yeast and warm water in a 1-cup glass measuring cup; let stand 5 minutes.

2. Meanwhile, whisk together flour and next 4 ingredients in a large bowl; cut in shortening and butter with a pastry blender until crumbly.

3. Combine yeast mixture and buttermilk, and add to flour mixture, stirring just until dry ingredients are moistened. Turn dough out onto a lightly floured surface, and knead about 1 minute.

4. Roll dough to ½-inch thickness. Cut with a 2-inch round cutter or into 2-inch squares. Place on 2 ungreased baking sheets.

5. Bake at 400° for 12 to 15 minutes or until golden.

Try This Twist!

cinnamon-raisin angel biscuits: Substitute ¼ cup firmly packed brown sugar for 2 Tbsp. sugar. Stir 1 cup baking raisins, 2 tsp. lemon zest, and 1 tsp. ground cinnamon into flour mixture in Step 2. Proceed with recipe as directed.

note: We tested with Sun-Maid Baking Raisins.

rejuvenated

20

up-a-notch sausage and gravy

Serve the Up-a-notch Sausage and Gravy over Angel Biscuits (page 20) or your favorite store-bought biscuits.

makes: 3 cups   hands-on time: 30 min.   total time: 30 min.

½   (1-lb.) package mild ground pork sausage

Butter, melted (optional)

1   (4-oz.) package fresh shiitake mushrooms, stemmed and sliced

2   shallots, minced

¼   cup all-purpose flour

½   cup chicken broth

¼   cup dry sherry or white wine

2   cups half-and-half

2   Tbsp. chopped fresh parsley

1   Tbsp. chopped fresh sage

1   tsp. Worcestershire sauce

½   tsp. salt

½   tsp. freshly ground pepper

1. Cook sausage in a large heavy skillet over medium-high heat, stirring often, 3 to 5 minutes or until sausage crumbles and is no longer pink; drain, reserving ¼ cup drippings in skillet. (If necessary, add melted butter to drippings to equal ¼ cup.)

2. Sauté mushrooms and shallots in hot drippings over medium-high heat 4 to 5 minutes or until golden. Whisk flour into mushroom mixture, and cook over medium-high heat, whisking constantly, 1 minute or until lightly browned. Add chicken broth and sherry, and cook 2 minutes, stirring to loosen particles from bottom of skillet. Stir in sausage.

3. Gradually add half-and-half, and cook over medium heat, stirring constantly, 2 to 3 minutes or until thickened and bubbly. Stir in parsley and remaining 4 ingredients. Reduce heat to low, and cook, stirring occasionally, 5 minutes. Serve warm.

Flavorful Preserves

Serve any one of these fruit-and-herb mixtures with the Angel Biscuits on page 20 for a delicious classic.

Mint Pepper Jelly: Stir together ½ cup pepper jelly and 1½ tsp. chopped fresh mint. (pictured on page 21, bottom right)

Basil-Blackberry Preserves: Stir together ½ cup blackberry preserves and 1½ to 2 tsp. chopped fresh basil. (pictured on page 21, bottom right)

Rosemary-Pear Preserves: Stir together ½ cup pear preserves and ½ tsp. chopped fresh rosemary. (pictured on page 21, bottom right)

Balsamic-Strawberry Preserves: Bring ¾ cup balsamic vinegar to a boil in a saucepan over medium-high heat. Reduce heat to medium low, and simmer, stirring occasionally, 18 to 20 minutes or until reduced to about 2 Tbsp. Let cool 10 minutes. Stir in 1 cup strawberry preserves. (pictured on page 21, bottom right)

cornbread biscuits

makes: about 15 biscuits
hands-on time: 30 min.   total time: 53 min.

3   cups self-rising soft-wheat
    flour
½   cup yellow self-rising cornmeal
    mix
¼   cup cold butter, cut into
    pieces
¼   cup shortening, cut into pieces
1½ cups buttermilk
1   tsp. yellow cornmeal
2   Tbsp. butter, melted

1. Preheat oven to 500°. Whisk together first 2 ingredients in a large bowl. Cut in cold butter and shortening with a pastry blender until mixture resembles small peas and dough is crumbly. Cover and chill 10 minutes. Add buttermilk, stirring just until dry ingredients are moistened.

2. Turn dough out onto a heavily floured surface; knead 3 or 4 times. Pat dough into a ¾-inch-thick circle.

3. Cut dough with a well-floured 2½-inch round cutter, rerolling scraps as needed. Sprinkle cornmeal on ungreased baking sheets; place biscuits on baking sheets. Lightly brush tops with 2 Tbsp. melted butter.

4. Bake at 500° for 13 to 15 minutes or until golden brown.

note: We tested with White Lily Bleached Self-Rising Flour.

crispy chicken cutlets

These taste similar to the chicken from a certain closed-on-Sundays fast-food chain that folks love. The secret? Dill pickle juice!

makes: about 16 servings
hands-on time: 30 min.   total time: 8 hr., 30 min.

8   (4-oz.) chicken breast cutlets,
    cut in half crosswise
2   cups dill pickle juice from jar
2   large eggs
¾   cup self-rising cornmeal mix
¾   cup fine, dry breadcrumbs
¼   cup finely chopped fresh
    parsley
1   tsp. pepper
½   tsp. salt
1   cup peanut oil

1. Combine first 2 ingredients in a 1-gal. zip-top plastic freezer bag. Seal bag, pressing out most of air, and chill 8 hours.

2. Whisk together eggs and 3 Tbsp. water in a shallow bowl. Combine cornmeal mix and next 3 ingredients in a second shallow bowl. Remove chicken from marinade, discarding marinade; sprinkle chicken with salt. Dip chicken in egg mixture, and dredge in cornmeal mixture, pressing firmly to adhere.

3. Heat oil in a large nonstick skillet over medium-high heat. Add chicken, and cook, in batches, 2 to 3 minutes on each side or until done.

cinnamon rolls with cream cheese icing

Make sure the butter you spread on the rolled out dough is very soft.

makes: 16 rolls
hands-on time: 30 min.   total time: 3 hr., 40 min., including icing

1   (¼-oz.) envelope active dry yeast
¼   cup warm water (105° to 115°)
1   tsp. granulated sugar
½   cup butter, softened
1   cup granulated sugar, divided
1   tsp. salt
2   large eggs, lightly beaten
1   cup milk
1   Tbsp. fresh lemon juice
4½ cups bread flour
¼   tsp. ground nutmeg
¼   to ½ cup bread flour
1   cup chopped pecans
½   cup very soft butter
½   cup firmly packed light brown sugar
1   Tbsp. ground cinnamon
Cream Cheese Icing

1. Combine first 3 ingredients in a 1-cup glass measuring cup; let stand 5 minutes.

2. Beat ½ cup softened butter at medium speed with a heavy-duty electric stand mixer until creamy. Gradually add ½ cup granulated sugar and 1 tsp. salt, beating at medium speed until light and fluffy. Add eggs and next 2 ingredients, beating until blended. Stir in yeast mixture.

3. Combine 4½ cups bread flour and ¼ tsp. nutmeg. Gradually add flour mixture to butter mixture, beating at low speed 1 to 2 minutes or until well blended.

4. Sprinkle about ¼ cup bread flour onto a flat surface; turn dough out, and knead until smooth and elastic (about 5 minutes), adding up to ¼ cup bread flour as needed to prevent dough from sticking to hands and surface. Place dough in a lightly greased large bowl, turning to grease top. Cover and let rise in a warm place (85°), free from drafts, 1½ to 2 hours or until doubled in bulk.

5. Meanwhile, preheat oven to 350°. Bake pecans in a single layer 8 to 10 minutes or until toasted and fragrant, stirring halfway through.

6. Punch dough down; turn out onto a lightly floured surface. Roll into a 16- x 12-inch rectangle. Spread with ½ cup very soft butter, leaving a 1-inch border around edges. (Butter should be very soft so dough will not tear.) Stir together brown sugar, cinnamon, and remaining ½ cup granulated sugar, and sprinkle sugar mixture over butter. Top with pecans.

7. Roll up dough, jelly-roll fashion, starting at 1 long side; cut into 16 slices (about 1 inch thick). Place rolls, cut sides down, in 2 lightly greased 10-inch round pans.

8. Cover and let rise in a warm place (85°), free from drafts, 1 hour or until doubled in bulk. Preheat oven to 350°. Bake at 350° for 20 to 22 minutes or until rolls are golden brown. Cool in pans 5 minutes. Brush warm rolls with Cream Cheese Icing. Serve immediately.

cream cheese icing

makes: 1½ cups   hands-on time: 10 min.   total time: 10 min.

2 Tbsp. butter, softened
1 (3-oz.) package cream cheese, softened
2¼ cups powdered sugar
1 tsp. vanilla extract
2 Tbsp. milk, divided

1. Beat butter and cream cheese at medium speed with an electric mixer until creamy. Gradually add powdered sugar, beating at low speed until blended. Stir in vanilla and 1 Tbsp. milk. Add remaining 1 Tbsp. milk, 1 tsp. at a time, as needed, until icing is smooth and creamy.

Try These Twists!

apple-cinnamon rolls: Prepare recipe as directed through Step 5. Peel and chop 2 Granny Smith apples (about 3 cups chopped). Place apples in a small microwave-safe bowl, and pour 1 cup apple cider or apple juice over apples. Microwave at HIGH 5 minutes or until tender. Drain and cool 15 minutes. Proceed with recipe as directed, sprinkling apples over brown sugar mixture in Step 6 before topping with pecans. hands-on time: 30 min.; total time: 4 hr., including icing.

chocolate-cinnamon rolls: Prepare recipe as directed through Step 6 (do not top with pecans). Chop 2 (4-oz.) bittersweet chocolate baking bars. Sprinkle chocolate over brown sugar mixture. Top with pecans. Proceed as directed. hands-on time: 35 min.; total time: 3 hr., 45 min., including icing.

strawberry-lemonade muffins

These muffins taste great fresh from the oven and topped with Strawberry Curd.

makes: 15 muffins   hands-on time: 15 min.   total time: 42 min.

2½ cups self-rising flour
1¼ cups sugar, divided
1   (8-oz.) container sour cream
½ cup butter, melted
1   Tbsp. lemon zest
¼ cup fresh lemon juice
2   large eggs, lightly beaten
1½ cups diced fresh strawberries

1. Preheat oven to 400°. Combine flour and 1 cup sugar in a large bowl; make a well in center of mixture.

2. Stir together sour cream and next 4 ingredients; add to flour mixture, stirring just until dry ingredients are moistened. Gently fold strawberries into batter. Spoon batter into lightly greased 12-cup muffin pans, filling three-fourths full. Sprinkle remaining ¼ cup sugar over batter.

3. Bake at 400° for 16 to 18 minutes or until golden brown and a wooden pick inserted in center comes out clean. Cool in pans on a wire rack 1 minute; remove from pans to wire rack, and cool 10 minutes.

strawberry curd

makes: about 3⅓ cups
hands-on time: 30 min.   total time: 8 hr., 30 min.

4   cups sliced fresh strawberries
½ cup sugar
2   Tbsp. cornstarch
¼ cup fresh lime juice
3   large eggs
2   egg yolks
3   Tbsp. butter

1. Process strawberries in a blender or food processor until smooth, stopping to scrape down sides as needed. Press strawberries through a large wire-mesh strainer into a medium bowl, using back of a spoon to squeeze out juice; discard pulp and seeds.

2. Combine sugar and cornstarch in a 3-qt. saucepan; gradually whisk in strawberry puree and lime juice. Whisk in 3 large eggs and 2 egg yolks. Bring mixture to a boil over medium heat, whisking constantly, and cook, whisking constantly, 1 minute. Remove from heat, and whisk in butter. Place plastic wrap directly on warm curd (to prevent a film from forming); chill 8 hours. Serve with hot biscuits, Strawberry-Lemonade Muffins, or use as a filling for tart shells.

PUMPKINS

You know that fall has arrived in the South at the first sightings of pumpkins for sale at the grocery store and farmers' markets. Then it's time to pull out those favorite recipes for pies, breads, and other baked goods. When choosing pumpkins, look for small ones, about 5 to 8 pounds, with tough skin. They're prized for their concentrated flavor and sweetness. Also make sure that the pumpkin is firm all the way around. If the bottom or stem end gives at all when pressed, it's past prime. Store it in the refrigerator for up to 3 months or in a cool, dry place for up to 1 month. Once cut, wrap the pumpkin tightly in plastic wrap, refrigerate, and use within 3 to 4 days.

If you've ever carved a jack-o'-lantern, you know how to tackle a fresh pumpkin. Use your hand or a spoon to remove the seeds and stringy flesh. You can also go beyond traditional pumpkin dishes; quarter, steam, and mash the flesh, mixing it with black pepper or brown sugar to serve as a side dish. For a healthy snack, consider roasting the seeds.

sticky-bun pumpkin muffins

makes: 2 dozen   hands-on time: 20 min.   total time: 1 hr.

2   cups pecan halves and pieces
½   cup butter, melted
½   cup firmly packed light
     brown sugar
2   Tbsp. light corn syrup
3½   cups all-purpose flour
3   cups granulated sugar
1   Tbsp. pumpkin pie spice
1   tsp. baking soda
1   tsp. salt
1   (15-oz.) can pumpkin
1   cup canola oil
4   large eggs

1. Preheat oven to 350°. Bake pecans in a single layer in a shallow pan 8 to 10 minutes or until toasted and fragrant, stirring halfway through.

2. Stir together melted butter and next 2 ingredients. Spoon 1 rounded teaspoonful butter mixture into each cup of 2 lightly greased 12-cup muffin pans, and top each with 1 rounded table-spoonful pecans.

3. Stir together flour and next 4 ingredients in a large bowl, and make a well in center of mixture. Whisk together pumpkin, next 2 ingredients, and ⅔ cup water; add to dry ingredients, stirring just until moistened.

4. Spoon batter into prepared muffin pans, filling three-fourths full.

5. Bake at 350° for 25 to 30 minutes or until a wooden pick inserted in center comes out clean. Invert pan immediately to remove muffins, and arrange muffins on a wire rack. Spoon any topping remaining in muffin cups over muffins. Let cool 5 minutes.

Try This Twist!

pecan-pumpkin bread: Omit butter, brown sugar, and corn syrup. Substitute 1½ cups chopped pecans for 2 cups pecan halves and pieces; toast as directed in Step 1. Omit Step 2. Prepare batter as directed in Step 3; stir in pecans. Spoon batter into 2 greased and floured 9- x 5-inch loaf pans. Bake at 350° for 1 hour to 1 hour and 10 minutes or until a long wooden pick inserted in center comes out clean. Cool in pans on a wire rack 10 minutes. Remove from pans to wire rack, and cool completely (about 1 hour). makes: 2 loaves; hands-on time: 20 min.; total time: 2 hr., 40 min.

peach-pecan muffins

makes: 12 muffins   hands-on time: 10 min.   total time: 45 min.

1½ cups all-purpose flour
½ cup granulated sugar
2 tsp. baking powder
1 tsp. ground cinnamon
¼ tsp. salt
½ cup butter, melted
¼ cup milk
1 large egg
1 cup frozen sliced peaches, thawed and diced
12 paper baking cups
Vegetable cooking spray
Pecan Streusel

1. Preheat oven to 400°. Combine flour and next 4 ingredients in a large bowl; make a well in center of mixture. Stir together butter, milk, and egg; add to dry ingredients, stirring just until moistened. Gently stir in peaches.

2. Place paper baking cups in 1 (12-cup) muffin pan, and coat with cooking spray; spoon batter into cups, filling two-thirds full. Sprinkle with Pecan Streusel.

3. Bake at 400° for 20 to 25 minutes or until a wooden pick inserted in center comes out clean. Cool in pan on a wire rack 10 minutes; remove from pan, and serve warm or at room temperature.

pecan streusel

makes: topping for 12 muffins
hands-on time: 5 min. total time: 5 min.

½ cup chopped pecans
⅓ cup firmly packed brown sugar
¼ cup all-purpose flour
2 Tbsp. melted butter
1 tsp. ground cinnamon

1. Stir together pecans and next 4 ingredients until crumbly. Use as topping for muffins as directed.

spiced peach-carrot bread

makes: 1 loaf   hands-on time: 15 min.   total time: 2 hr., 50 min.

¾   cup chopped pecans
2½ cups all-purpose flour
1   cup sugar
1   tsp. ground cinnamon
¾   tsp. baking soda
½   tsp. baking powder
½   tsp. salt
¼   tsp. ground nutmeg
1½ cups peeled and chopped
    fresh, ripe peaches
¾   cup freshly grated carrots
⅔   cup vegetable oil
½   cup milk
2   large eggs, lightly beaten

1. Preheat oven to 350°. Bake pecans in a single layer in a shallow pan 8 to 10 minutes or until toasted and fragrant, stirring halfway through. Cool 15 minutes.

2. Stir together flour and next 6 ingredients in a large bowl; add peaches, next 4 ingredients, and toasted pecans, stirring just until dry ingredients are moistened. Spoon batter into a lightly greased 9- x 5-inch loaf pan.

3. Bake at 350° for 1 hour and 5 minutes to 1 hour and 10 minutes or until a long wooden pick inserted in center comes out clean. Cool in pan on a wire rack 5 minutes. Remove from pan to wire rack, and cool completely (about 1 hour).

TASTE OF SUMMER

PEACHES

There's nothing quite like biting into a ripe, juicy peach that's been handpicked straight into a bushel basket. Look for fruit that's firm with a taut, unblemished skin and no signs of bruising or wrinkles. And if you smell peaches when you walk up to the stand, you'll know that they're ripe.

baked toasted-pecan pancake with caramel-apple topping

Use a light hand when stirring the batter; overmixing will create a rubbery texture.

makes: 6 to 8 servings
hands-on time: 15 min.   total time: 56 min., including topping

1   cup chopped pecans
1¾ cups all-purpose flour
2   tsp. sugar
1½ tsp. baking powder
1   tsp. baking soda
½   tsp. salt
2   cups buttermilk
2   large eggs
¼   cup butter, melted
Caramel-Apple Topping
Powdered sugar

1. Preheat oven to 350°. Bake pecans in a single layer in a shallow pan 4 to 5 minutes or until lightly toasted, stirring halfway through. Cool 10 minutes.

2. Meanwhile, combine flour and next 4 ingredients in a large bowl. Whisk together buttermilk and eggs. Gradually stir buttermilk mixture into flour mixture. Gently stir in butter. (Batter will be lumpy.)

3. Pour batter into a lightly greased 15- x 10-inch jelly-roll pan. Sprinkle with pecans.

4. Bake at 350° for 25 to 30 minutes or until golden brown and a wooden pick inserted into center comes out clean. Serve immediately with warm Caramel-Apple Topping and powdered sugar.

caramel-apple topping

makes: about 3 cups
hands-on time: 15 min.   total time: 15 min.

2   (12-oz.) packages frozen spiced apples, thawed
½   cup firmly packed brown sugar
2   Tbsp. butter
1   tsp. vanilla extract
¼   tsp. salt

1. Stir together all ingredients in a medium saucepan. Bring to a boil over medium heat, stirring occasionally; reduce heat to low, and simmer, stirring occasionally, 2 to 3 minutes or until thoroughly heated.

note: We tested with Stouffer's Harvest Apples.

lemon-poppy seed Belgian waffles with blackberry maple syrup

makes: 4 servings
hands-on time: 25 min.   total time: 30 min., including syrup

2   cups all-purpose baking mix
1   to 2 Tbsp. poppy seeds
1   Tbsp. lemon zest
1¼ cups cold club soda
1   large egg, lightly beaten
¼   cup butter, melted
Blackberry Maple Syrup
Crème fraîche (optional)
Garnish: fresh mint sprigs

1. Stir together baking mix, poppy seeds, and lemon zest. Whisk together club soda, egg, and butter in a small bowl; gently whisk egg mixture into poppy seed mixture. (Mixture will be lumpy.) Let stand 3 minutes.

2. Cook batter in a preheated, oiled Belgian-style waffle iron until golden (about ¾ to 1 cup batter each). Serve with Blackberry Maple Syrup and, if desired, crème fraîche. Garnish, if desired.

note: If you don't have a Belgian-style waffle iron, use ½ cup batter for each waffle in a traditional waffle iron.

blackberry maple syrup

makes: 2 cups   hands-on time: 5 min.   total time: 5 min.

½   cup maple syrup
1   (12-oz.) package frozen blackberries*
1   tsp. lemon zest
2   tsp. lemon juice

1. Combine all ingredients in a medium bowl.

* Frozen mixed berries, thawed, may be substituted.

Try This Twist!

lemon-poppy seed pancakes: Prepare batter as directed. Pour about ¼ cup batter for each pancake onto a hot, lightly greased griddle or large nonstick skillet. Cook pancakes 3 to 4 minutes or until tops are covered with bubbles and edges look dry and cooked; turn and cook other side.

praline-pecan french toast (pictured on opposite page)

makes: 8 to 10 servings
hands-on time: 20 min.   total time: 8 hr., 55 min.

1   (16-oz.) French bread loaf
1   cup firmly packed light brown
    sugar
⅓   cup butter, melted
2   Tbsp. maple syrup
¾   cup chopped pecans
4   large eggs, lightly beaten
1   cup 2% reduced-fat milk
2   Tbsp. granulated sugar
1   tsp. ground cinnamon
1   tsp. vanilla extract

1. Cut 10 (1-inch-thick) slices of bread. Reserve remaining bread for another use.

2. Stir together brown sugar and next 2 ingredients; pour into a lightly greased 13- x 9-inch baking dish. Sprinkle with chopped pecans.

3. Whisk together eggs and next 4 ingredients. Arrange bread slices over pecans; pour egg mixture over bread. Cover and chill 8 hours.

4. Preheat oven to 350°. Bake bread at 350° for 35 to 37 minutes or until golden brown. Serve immediately.

sparkling ginger-orange cocktails
(pictured on page 13, bottom right)

makes: about 23 cups
hands-on time: 10 min.   total time: 10 min.

1   Tbsp. finely grated ginger
2   (750-milliliter) bottles chilled
    sparkling wine
1   (89-oz.) container orange
    juice
1   (46-oz.) can chilled pineapple
    juice
Garnish: orange slices, fresh mint

1. Place ginger in a piece of cheesecloth, and squeeze juice from ginger into a large pitcher; discard cheesecloth.

2. Stir sparkling wine and juices into ginger juice. Serve over ice. Garnish, if desired.

note: We tested with Freixenet Spumante for sparkling wine.

NOSTALGIC

baked Tex-Mex pimiento cheese dip

makes: about 4 cups
hands-on time: 15 min.   total time: 35 min.

1½ cups mayonnaise
½ (12-oz.) jar roasted red bell peppers, drained and chopped
¼ cup chopped green onions
1 jalapeño pepper, seeded and minced
1 (8-oz.) block extra-sharp Cheddar cheese, shredded
1 (8-oz.) block pepper Jack cheese, shredded

1. Preheat oven to 350°. Stir together first 4 ingredients in a large bowl; stir in cheeses. Spoon mixture into a lightly greased 2-qt. baking dish.

2. Bake at 350° for 20 to 25 minutes or until dip is golden and bubbly. Serve with French bread cubes.

cheese and bacon okra poppers

(pictured on opposite page)

We loved the bacon-wrapped pods, but you can save prep time by crumbling the bacon into the cheese mixture, stuffing the pods, and baking.

makes: 16 servings   hands-on time: 20 min.   total time: 44 min.

16 bacon slices
1 lb. fresh okra (32 pods)
1 (8-oz.) container chive-and-onion cream cheese, softened
½ cup shredded extra-sharp Cheddar cheese
¼ cup chopped green onions
¼ tsp. kosher salt
¼ tsp. freshly ground pepper
Vegetable cooking spray

1. Preheat oven to 425° with oven rack 6 inches from heat. Cook bacon, in 2 batches, in a large skillet over medium-high heat 1 to 2 minutes on each side or just until bacon begins to curl; remove bacon, and drain on paper towels. Cut each slice in half crosswise. Discard drippings.

2. Cut each okra pod lengthwise down 1 side, leaving stem and other side of pod intact; remove seeds and membranes.

3. Stir together cream cheese and next 4 ingredients in a small bowl. Carefully pipe cheese mixture into cavity of each okra pod. Wrap each stuffed okra pod with 1 bacon piece, and secure with a wooden pick.

4. Place half of okra, cheese side up, on a foil-lined baking sheet coated with cooking spray. Bake at 425° for 8 minutes or until okra is tender and bacon is crisp. Transfer to a serving platter; keep warm. Repeat procedure with remaining half of okra. Serve warm.

tiny tomato tarts

These tasty little treats are a great make-ahead appetizer or can also be served alongside a salad for a light supper.

makes: 24 tartlets   hands-on time: 30 min.   total time: 50 min.

½ (14.1-oz.) package refrigerated piecrusts
1 (14.5-oz.) can petite diced tomatoes
1 Tbsp. chopped fresh basil
Salt and freshly ground pepper to taste
⅔ cup mayonnaise
½ cup grated Parmesan cheese
¼ cup (1 oz.) freshly shredded Cheddar cheese
¼ cup (1 oz.) freshly shredded mozzarella cheese
Garnish: fresh basil leaves

1. Preheat oven to 425°. Unroll piecrust on a lightly floured surface; roll into a 12-inch circle. Cut into 24 rounds using a 2-inch scalloped-edge round cutter. Press rounds into bottoms of ungreased miniature muffin cups. (Dough will come slightly up sides, forming a cup.) Prick bottom of dough once with a fork.

2. Bake at 425° for 4 to 5 minutes or until set. Cool in pans on a wire rack 15 minutes. Reduce oven temperature to 350°.

3. Meanwhile, drain tomatoes well, pressing between paper towels. Combine tomatoes and chopped basil in a small bowl; season with salt and pepper to taste. Stir together mayonnaise and next 3 ingredients in a medium bowl. Divide tomato mixture among pastry shells, and top with mayonnaise mixture.

4. Bake at 350° for 18 to 20 minutes. Serve immediately. Garnish, if desired.

note: To make ahead, bake and cool pastry shells as directed in Steps 1 and 2. Remove from muffin pans, and store in an airtight container for up to 3 days. Return pastry shells to muffin pans, and fill and bake as directed.

zucchini bacon spoon bread

When making spoon bread, be sure to start with plain cornmeal and not a cornmeal mix, which contains flour, salt, and a leavening agent.

makes: 8 servings
hands-on time: 9 min.   total time: 1 hr., 10 min.

2   cups milk
1   Tbsp. sugar
1   tsp. salt
½   tsp. freshly ground pepper
⅛   tsp. ground red pepper
1   cup plain yellow cornmeal
2   cups shredded zucchini (about
    1 large)
1   cup (4 oz.) shredded sharp
    Cheddar cheese
8   cooked bacon slices, crumbled
2   large eggs, separated
Vegetable cooking spray

1. Preheat oven to 375°. Bring first 5 ingredients to a simmer in a large heavy saucepan over medium-high heat (do not boil); gradually whisk in cornmeal. Cook, stirring constantly, 1 minute or until thick and smooth. Remove from heat, and stir in zucchini, cheese, and bacon. Stir in egg yolks until blended.

2. Beat egg whites at high speed with an electric mixer until stiff peaks form. Stir one-third of egg white mixture into cornmeal mixture. Fold in remaining egg white mixture. Spoon into a 1½-qt. soufflé dish or deep baking dish coated with cooking spray.

3. Bake at 375° for 46 to 50 minutes or until top is lightly browned. Serve immediately.

sweet green tomato corn muffins

If you're looking for a new twist for this year's crop of green tomatoes, try this Southern favorite.

makes: about 2 dozen
hands-on time: 30 min.   total time: 45 min.

2   cups seeded, diced green
    tomatoes (about ¾ lb.)
½   cup sugar, divided
½   cup butter, melted and divided
2   cups self-rising white
    cornmeal mix
2   tsp. lemon zest
5   large eggs
1   (16-oz.) container sour cream
Vegetable cooking spray
Fresh Basil Butter (optional)

1. Preheat oven to 450°. Sauté tomatoes and 2 Tbsp. sugar in 2 Tbsp. melted butter in a large skillet over medium-high heat 10 to 12 minutes or until tomatoes begin to caramelize and turn light brown.

2. Stir together cornmeal mix, lemon zest, and remaining 6 Tbsp. sugar in a large bowl; make a well in center of mixture. Whisk together eggs, sour cream, and remaining 6 Tbsp. butter; add to cornmeal mixture, stirring just until dry ingredients are moistened. Fold in tomatoes.

3. Generously coat small (¼-cup) brioche molds or muffin pans with cooking spray; spoon batter into molds, filling two-thirds full. Bake at 450° for 15 to 17 minutes or until a wooden pick inserted in center comes out clean. Serve with Fresh Basil Butter, if desired.

fresh basil butter

makes: ½ cup   hands-on time: 5 min.   total time: 5 min.

½   cup softened butter
2   Tbsp. finely chopped fresh
    basil

1. Stir together butter and basil.

home-style green bean casserole

This essential holiday casserole gets a much-needed makeover from fresh veggies and a lightened, but super-rich homemade sauce.

makes: 8 servings
hands-on time: 25 min.   total time: 55 min.

1½ lb. fresh green beans, trimmed
2   Tbsp. butter
¼   cup all-purpose flour
1½ cups 2% reduced-fat milk
½   cup nonfat buttermilk
1   Tbsp. Ranch dressing mix
2   tsp. chopped fresh thyme
¼   tsp. salt
¼   tsp. pepper
1   tsp. butter
1   (8-oz.) package sliced fresh mushrooms
Vegetable cooking spray
1   cup French fried onions, crushed
½   cup panko (Japanese bread-crumbs)
2   plum tomatoes, seeded and chopped

1. Preheat oven to 350°. Cook green beans in boiling salted water to cover in a Dutch oven 4 to 6 minutes or to desired degree of doneness; drain. Plunge into ice water to stop the cooking process; drain and pat dry.

2. Melt 2 Tbsp. butter in Dutch oven over medium heat; whisk in flour until smooth. Cook, whisking constantly, 1 minute. Gradually whisk in 1½ cups milk; cook, whisking constantly, 3 to 4 minutes or until sauce is thickened and bubbly. Remove from heat, and whisk in buttermilk and next 4 ingredients.

3. Melt 1 tsp. butter in a medium skillet over medium-high heat; add mushrooms, and sauté 6 to 8 minutes or until lightly browned. Remove from heat; let stand 5 minutes. Gently toss mushrooms and green beans in buttermilk sauce. Place in a 13- x 9-inch or 3-qt. baking dish coated with cooking spray.

4. Combine French fried onions and next 2 ingredients; sprinkle over green bean mixture.

5. Bake at 350° for 25 to 30 minutes or until golden brown and bubbly. Serve immediately.

Southern-style collards (pictured on opposite page)

Hickory smoked salt adds a sizzling hit of pork-rich flavor (and zero fat grams) to thinly cut ribbons of greens.

makes: 8 servings   hands-on time: 30 min.   total time: 55 min.

2   bunches fresh collard greens (about 3 lb.)
1   large red onion, finely chopped
2   Tbsp. vegetable oil
2½ cups vegetable broth
¼   cup cider vinegar
2   Tbsp. dark brown sugar
1½ tsp. hickory smoked salt
½   tsp. dried crushed red pepper

1. Separate collard bunches into leaves. Trim and discard tough stalk from center of leaves; stack leaves, and roll up, starting at 1 long side. Cut roll into ⅛-inch-thick slices. Rinse slices under cold running water. Drain well.

2. Sauté onion in hot oil in a Dutch oven over medium-high heat 5 to 7 minutes or until tender. Add broth and next 4 ingredients. Bring to a boil.

3. Gradually add collards to Dutch oven, and cook, stirring occasionally, 6 to 8 minutes or just until wilted. Reduce heat to medium, and cook, stirring occasionally, 20 minutes or until tender.

nutty okra (pictured on page 61, top right)

makes: 4 servings   hands-on time: 22 min.   total time: 42 min.

1   lb. fresh okra, cut into ½-inch pieces
1   tsp. salt
1   egg white, lightly beaten
1   cup all-purpose baking mix
½   cup finely chopped salted dry-roasted peanuts
½   tsp. pepper
Peanut oil

1. Toss okra with salt, and let stand 20 minutes. Add egg white, stirring to coat. Stir together baking mix and next 2 ingredients in a large bowl. Add okra, tossing to coat; gently press peanut mixture onto okra, shaking off excess.

2. Pour oil to depth of 2 inches into a Dutch oven or cast-iron skillet; heat to 375°. Fry okra, in batches, 2 to 4 minutes or until golden; drain on paper towels.

Planting Tomatoes

I garden now because I want to, but when I was growing up, the family garden was a necessity. Money was tight, so every summer, my mother canned green beans, jellies, preserves, and chili sauce and filled a huge freezer with peas, corn, okra, squash, butter beans, and tomato sauce. The freezer occupied a corner of the dining room because we didn't have any other place to put it. (Undaunted, Mama learned to decorate around it at Christmas and Thanksgiving.) The garden we shared with Aunt Joyce and Aunt Patsy fed three families, and it was so big that my uncle had to break it up and lay off the rows with a tractor every spring. Planting it was an all-day chore, the only redeeming part of which was making mud holes for the tomatoes. Because you have to plant them deep, Daddy or my uncle would dig a big hole for each one and set a single plant in it. My cousin Kathy and I were charged with taking the garden hose and filling each hole with water, and then holding the tomato plant upright and piling mud around it. It was a squishy, messy enterprise, which we loved because it afforded us the opportunity to squirt each other with the hose and cover ourselves with cool mud on a hot day. So I guess you could say that, while we learned to plant tomatoes, we inadvertently invented the day spa—or at least, a country girl's version of it.

VFL

fried green tomatoes

Full of fresh, tangy flavor, fried green tomatoes are crusty on the outside and juicy on the inside. The secret for success is to use firm green tomatoes and shallow oil of about ½-inch depth.

makes: 6 servings
hands-on time: 30 min.   total time: 30 min.

1	large egg, lightly beaten	
½	cup buttermilk	
½	cup self-rising cornmeal mix	
½	tsp. salt	
½	tsp. pepper	
½	cup all-purpose flour	

3   medium-size, firm green tomatoes, cut into ⅓-inch-thick slices (about 1¼ lb.)

Vegetable oil

Salt to taste

1. Whisk together egg and buttermilk. Combine cornmeal mix, salt, pepper, and ¼ cup flour in a shallow dish. Dredge tomato slices in remaining ¼ cup flour, dip in egg mixture, and dredge in cornmeal mixture.

2. Pour oil to depth of ½ inch in a large cast-iron skillet; heat to 375° over medium-high heat. Fry tomatoes, in batches, in hot oil 2 minutes on each side or until golden. Drain on paper towels. Sprinkle hot tomatoes with salt to taste.

classic Southern dishes

scalloped sweet potato stacks

Each muffin cup flares slightly, so place slices from ends of potatoes in the bottom, and use wider slices from the middle of the potato at the top. We also like this with **Gruyère** instead of mozzarella.

makes: 12 servings
hands-on time: 25 min.   total time: 1 hr., 5 min.

1½ lb. small sweet
    potatoes, peeled and
    thinly sliced
2   tsp. chopped
    fresh thyme, divided
1   cup (4 oz.) freshly
    shredded mozzarella
    cheese, divided*
⅔   cup heavy cream
1   garlic clove, pressed
½   to ¾ tsp. salt
¼   tsp. freshly
    ground pepper
Garnish: fresh thyme

1. Preheat oven to 375°. Layer half of sweet potatoes in a lightly greased 12-cup muffin pan. Sprinkle with 1½ tsp. thyme and ½ cup cheese. Top with remaining sweet potatoes. (Potatoes will come slightly above the rim of each cup.)

2. Microwave cream, next 3 ingredients, and remaining ½ tsp. thyme in a microwave-safe bowl at HIGH 1 minute. Pour cream mixture into muffin cups (about 1 Tbsp. per cup).

3. Bake at 375°, covered with aluminum foil, 30 minutes. Uncover and sprinkle with remaining ½ cup cheese. Bake 5 to 7 minutes or until cheese is melted and slightly golden.

4. Let stand 5 minutes. Run a sharp knife around rim of each cup, and lift potato stacks from cups using a spoon or thin spatula. Transfer to a serving platter. Garnish, if desired.

*Gruyère cheese may be substituted.

SWEET POTATOES

While a Southern Thanksgiving just wouldn't be the same without a delicious sweet potato casserole topped with toasty marshmallows, browned pecans or both, this classic fall vegetable also tastes great in pies, biscuits, fries, soups, and more. When purchasing sweet potatoes, look for small to medium-size tubers with smooth skin and few bruises. Store them in a cool, dry, dark place. If the temperature is right (about 55°), you can keep them 3 to 4 weeks. Otherwise, you need to use them within a week. Do not refrigerate them.

Y'ALL ENJOY

Vegetable Plate

6 servings

Black-eyed Pea Cakes with Heirloom Tomatoes and Slaw
Baked Smokin' Macaroni and Cheese *(page 63)*
Nutty Okra *(page 55)*
Brown Sugar-Cinnamon Peach Pie *(page 80)*

---

black-eyed pea cakes with heirloom tomatoes and slaw (pictured on opposite page, bottom left)

makes: 6 servings   hands-on time: 20 min.   total time: 20 min.

1 (15-oz.) can seasoned black-eyed peas, undrained
2 garlic cloves, pressed
1 (6-oz.) package buttermilk cornbread mix
1 large egg, lightly beaten
¼ cup sour cream
1½ tsp. Southwest chipotle salt-free seasoning blend
1 tsp. salt, divided
⅓ cup sour cream
1 tsp. lime zest
1 Tbsp. fresh lime juice
2 tsp. sugar
1 (12-oz.) package fresh broccoli slaw
2 large beefsteak tomatoes, cut into ¼-inch-thick slices
Salt and freshly ground pepper to taste

1. Coarsely mash peas with a fork. Stir in garlic, next 4 ingredients, and ½ tsp. salt. Stir until blended.

2. Spoon about ¼ cup batter for each cake onto a hot, lightly greased griddle. Cook cakes 2 minutes or until edges look dry and cooked; turn and cook 2 more minutes.

3. Stir together ⅓ cup sour cream, next 3 ingredients, and remaining ½ tsp. salt in a large bowl. Stir in slaw.

4. Place each cooked cake on a serving plate; layer each with tomato slice and remaining cake. Season with salt and pepper to taste. Top with slaw; serve immediately.

nostalgic

60

baked smokin' macaroni and cheese

makes: 8 servings   hands-on time: 25 min.   total time: I hr.

1 lb. uncooked cellentani (corkscrew) pasta
2 Tbsp. butter
¼ cup all-purpose flour
3 cups milk
1 (12-oz.) can evaporated milk
1 cup (4 oz.) shredded smoked Gouda cheese
½ cup (2 oz.) shredded sharp Cheddar cheese
3 oz. cream cheese, softened
½ tsp. salt
¼ tsp. ground red pepper, divided
1 (8-oz.) package chopped smoked ham
Vegetable cooking spray
1¼ cups cornflakes cereal, crushed
1 Tbsp. butter, melted

1. Preheat oven to 350°. Prepare cellentani pasta according to package directions.

2. Meanwhile, melt 2 Tbsp. butter in a Dutch oven over medium heat. Gradually whisk in flour; cook, whisking constantly, 1 minute. Gradually whisk in milk and evaporated milk until smooth; cook, whisking constantly, 8 to 10 minutes or until slightly thickened. Whisk in Gouda cheese, next 3 ingredients, and ⅛ tsp. ground red pepper until smooth. Remove from heat, and stir in ham and pasta.

3. Pour pasta mixture into a 13- x 9-inch baking dish coated with cooking spray. Stir together crushed cereal, 1 Tbsp. melted butter, and remaining ⅛ tsp. ground red pepper; sprinkle over pasta mixture.

4. Bake at 350° for 30 minutes or until golden and bubbly. Let stand 5 minutes before serving.

note: We tested with Barilla Cellentani pasta and Cabot sharp Cheddar cheese.

Try These Twists!

pepper Jack macaroni and cheese: Substitute 1½ cups pepper Jack cheese for Gouda and Cheddar cheeses. Omit ground red pepper, if desired. Stir 1 (4.5-oz.) can chopped green chiles into pasta mixture.

sweet pea-and-prosciutto macaroni and cheese: Omit ham. Sauté 2 oz. thin prosciutto slices, cut into thin strips, in a small skillet over medium-high heat 2 minutes or until slightly browned. Stir prosciutto and 1 cup frozen sweet peas, thawed, into pasta mixture.

pimiento macaroni and cheese: Substitute 1½ cups sharp Cheddar cheese for Gouda and Cheddar cheeses. Stir 1 (4-oz.) jar diced pimiento, drained, into pasta mixture.

classic Southern dishes

pickled okra and shrimp salad

The sweet-hot pickled okra adds a zesty twist to this classic Southern salad. Serve it alongside fresh tomatoes or lettuce.

makes: 6 servings   hands-on time: 10 min.   total time: 40 min.

1   (3-oz.) package boil-in-bag shrimp-and-crab boil
1½ lb. peeled and deveined, medium-size raw shrimp
½   cup sliced sweet-hot pickled okra
1   (4-oz.) jar diced pimiento, drained
⅓   cup mayonnaise
3   Tbsp. minced red onion
½   tsp. lime zest
3   Tbsp. fresh lime juice
¼   tsp. pepper
⅛   tsp. salt
3   large avocados, sliced

1. Bring 8 cups water to a boil in a 3-qt. saucepan; add crab boil, and cook 5 minutes. Add shrimp; cover, remove from heat, and let stand 10 minutes or just until shrimp turn pink. Drain and cool 10 minutes.

2. Meanwhile, combine pickled okra, diced pimiento, and next 6 ingredients. Add shrimp, and serve immediately with avocado slices, or cover and chill until ready to serve.

note: We tested with Wickles pickled okra.

TASTE OF SPRING

AVOCADO

It's hard to think of the avocado as a fruit—a berry, in fact, marked by a single large seed—partly because it's so often used in salads, sandwiches, and other savory dishes. Yet between its nutty, subtle taste and buttery, sensuous texture, the avocado distinguishes itself as one of nature's most sublime fruits.

Texas toast tomato sandwiches

(pictured on opposite page)

makes: 6 servings   hands-on time: 15 min.   total time: 15 min.

1   (9.5-oz.) package five-cheese
     Texas toast
2   lb. assorted heirloom
     tomatoes
¼   cup bottled blue cheese
     vinaigrette
6   Tbsp. torn fresh basil
Salt and freshly ground pepper to
     taste
Garnishes: crumbled blue cheese,
     fresh basil leaves

1. Prepare Texas toast according to package directions.

2. Meanwhile, halve larger tomatoes, and cut into ¼-inch-thick slices; halve or quarter smaller tomatoes. Gently toss tomatoes with vinaigrette, basil, and salt and pepper to taste. Serve immediately over hot Texas toast. Garnish, if desired.

note: We tested with Pepperidge Farm Five Cheese Texas Toast.

cobb salad sandwiches

makes: 4 to 6 servings
hands-on time: 15 min.   total time: 25 min.

1   (12-oz.) French bread loaf
Avocado Mayonnaise
6   oz. smoked turkey slices
6   oz. honey-maple ham slices
6   (1-oz.) Swiss cheese slices
8   cooked bacon slices
2   hard-cooked eggs, sliced
1   tomato, sliced
2   cups arugula
Salt
Pepper

1. Cut French bread loaf in half horizontally; scoop out soft bread from center of each half, leaving a ½-inch-thick shell to make filling the sandwich easier. Reserve soft bread for another use.

2. Spread inside of bread shells with Avocado Mayonnaise. Layer bottom shell with turkey, ham, Swiss cheese, bacon, sliced eggs, sliced tomato, and arugula. Season with salt and pepper. Top with remaining bread shell. Cut into sandwiches.

Avocado Mayonnaise: Process 1 avocado, coarsely chopped; ¾ cup mayonnaise; 1 jalapeño pepper, seeded and chopped; 2 Tbsp. fresh cilantro leaves; and 2 Tbsp. fresh lime juice in a food processor until smooth. Season with salt to taste. Makes: about 1 cup.

classic Southern dishes

67

goat cheese and strawberry grilled cheese (pictured at right, front left)

makes: 3 servings
hands-on time: 20 min.   total time: 20 min.

1	(4-oz.) goat cheese log, softened	
6	whole grain bread slices	
4½	tsp. red pepper jelly	
¾	cup sliced fresh strawberries	

6   large fresh basil leaves
1½ cups fresh watercress or arugula
Salt and freshly ground pepper to taste

1. Spread goat cheese on 1 side of 3 bread slices. Spread pepper jelly on 1 side of remaining bread slices; layer with strawberries, basil leaves, and watercress. Sprinkle with salt and pepper to taste. Top with remaining bread, goat cheese sides down. Cook sandwiches in a large, lightly greased nonstick skillet over medium heat 2 to 3 minutes on each side or until golden brown.

chilled avocado soup with fresh corn relish (pictured at left, back right)

makes: 6 servings
hands-on time: 24 min.
total time: 1 hr., 34 min., including relish

4 ripe avocados, peeled and quartered	1 (8-oz.) container sour cream
1 tsp. salt	¼ cup Johannisberg Riesling
1 tsp. green hot sauce	3 Tbsp. fresh lime juice
1 (14-oz) can chicken broth	Fresh Corn Relish
1½ cups half-and-half	

1. Process avocados and next 3 ingredients in a blender or food processor until smooth, stopping to scrape down sides. Pour mixture into a large bowl; stir in half-and-half and next 3 ingredients until smooth. Place plastic wrap directly on soup; chill 1 hour.

2. Serve soup with relish.

note: Any off-dry white wines, such as Gewürztraminer or Chenin Blanc, may be substituted for the Riesling.

fresh corn relish

makes: 1½ cups
hands-on time: 10 min.   total time: 1 hr., 10 min.

2 Tbsp. sherry vinegar	1 tsp. salt
1 Tbsp. extra virgin olive oil	¾ cup fresh corn kernels (1½ ears)
1 Tbsp. chopped fresh cilantro	½ cup diced tomato
1 tsp. freshly ground pepper	¼ cup chopped red onion

1. Whisk together first 5 ingredients in a medium bowl. Stir in corn kernels, tomato, and onion. Cover and chill 1 hour.

classic Southern dishes

chicken cobbler casserole

This dish combines the robust flavors and cheesy bread topping of French onion soup with chicken pot pie.

makes: 4 servings   hands-on time: 35 min.   total time: 50 min.

6   Tbsp. melted butter, divided
4   cups cubed sourdough rolls
⅓   cup grated Parmesan cheese
2   Tbsp. chopped fresh parsley
2   medium-size sweet onions, sliced
1   (8-oz.) package sliced fresh mushrooms
1   cup white wine
1   (10¾-oz.) can cream of mushroom soup
½   cup drained and chopped jarred roasted red bell peppers
2½ cups shredded cooked chicken

1. Preheat oven to 400°. Toss 4 Tbsp. melted butter with next 3 ingredients, and set aside.

2. Sauté onions in remaining 2 Tbsp. butter in a large skillet over medium-high heat 15 minutes or until golden brown. Add mushrooms, and sauté 5 minutes.

3. Stir in wine and next 3 ingredients; cook, stirring constantly, 5 minutes or until bubbly. Spoon mixture into a lightly greased 9-inch square baking dish or 3 (10-oz.) ramekins; top evenly with bread mixture.

4. Bake at 400° for 15 minutes or until golden brown.

double-crust chicken pot pie

makes: 6 to 8 servings
hands-on time: 31 min.   total time: 1 hr., 46 min.

½ cup butter
2   medium leeks, sliced
½ cup all-purpose flour
1   (14-oz.) can chicken broth
3   cups chopped cooked chicken
1½ cups frozen cubed
     hashbrowns with onions and
     peppers
1   cup matchstick carrots
⅓ cup chopped fresh flat-leaf
     parsley
½ tsp. salt
½ tsp. freshly ground pepper
1   (17.3-oz.) package frozen puff
     pastry sheets, thawed
1   large egg

1. Preheat oven to 375°. Melt butter in a large skillet over medium heat; add leeks, and sauté 3 minutes. Sprinkle with flour; cook, stirring constantly, 3 minutes. Whisk in chicken broth; bring to a boil, whisking constantly. Remove from heat; stir in chicken and next 5 ingredients.

2. Roll each pastry sheet into a 12- x 10-inch rectangle on a lightly floured surface. Fit 1 sheet into a 9-inch deep-dish pie plate; spoon chicken mixture into pastry. Place remaining pastry sheet over filling in opposite direction of bottom sheet; fold edges under, and press with tines of a fork, sealing to bottom crust. Whisk together egg and 1 Tbsp. water, and brush over top of pie.

3. Bake at 375° on lower oven rack 55 to 60 minutes or until browned. Let stand 15 minutes.

TASTE OF SUMMER

CARROTS

Choose carrots that are firm and brightly colored, avoiding ones that are cracked. If the leafy tops are attached, make sure they're not wilted. To store them, remove the tops if attached; place them in plastic bags, and refrigerate for up to 2 weeks. To prepare them, wash and cut the carrots into sticks for dipping and eating, or shred them to add to recipes.

herbed tomato tart

We used basil, dill, thyme, and parsley, but just about any combination of herbs that pair well with tomatoes—such as oregano and tarragon—would work.

makes: 6 servings
hands-on time: 25 min.   total time: 1 hr., 23 min.

2   medium tomatoes, thinly sliced
     (about ¾ lb.)
½   pt. assorted small tomatoes,
     halved
¾   tsp. salt, divided
1   (17.3-oz.) package frozen puff
     pastry sheets, thawed
1   (8-oz.) package shredded
     mozzarella cheese
1   (4-oz.) package crumbled feta
     cheese
¼   cup finely chopped chives
1   garlic clove, minced
¼   cup finely chopped assorted
     fresh herbs
1   Tbsp. olive oil
Garnish: fresh herbs

1. Preheat oven to 400°. Place tomatoes in a single layer on paper towels; sprinkle with ½ tsp. salt. Let stand 30 minutes. Pat dry with paper towels.

2. Meanwhile, roll 1 pastry sheet into a 14-inch square on a lightly floured surface; place on an ungreased baking sheet. Cut 4 (12- x 1-inch) strips from remaining pastry sheet, and place strips along outer edges of pastry square, forming a border. Reserve remaining pastry for another use.

3. Bake at 400° for 14 minutes or until browned.

4. Sprinkle pastry with mozzarella cheese and next 3 ingredients. Top with tomatoes in a single layer. Sprinkle tomatoes with herbs and remaining ¼ tsp. salt; drizzle with oil.

5. Bake at 400° for 14 to 15 minutes or until cheese melts. Serve immediately. Garnish, if desired.

hamburger steak with sweet onion-mushroom gravy

This beef recipe makes the most of your busy weeknights. You can make the patties ahead, then simply thaw in the fridge overnight before using.

makes: 4 servings   hands-on time: 15 min.   total time: 35 min.

2   honey wheat bread slices
1   lb. ground round
1   large egg, lightly beaten
2   garlic cloves, minced
½   tsp. salt
½   tsp. freshly ground pepper
1   (1.2-oz.) envelope brown gravy mix
1   Tbsp. vegetable oil
1   (8-oz.) package sliced fresh mushrooms
1   medium-size sweet onion, halved and thinly sliced

1. Process bread slices in a food processor 10 seconds or until finely chopped. Place breadcrumbs in a mixing bowl; add ground round and next 4 ingredients. Gently combine until blended, using your hands. Shape into 4 (4-inch) patties.

2. Whisk together brown gravy mix and 1½ cups water.

3. Cook patties in hot oil in a large skillet over medium-high heat 2 minutes on each side or just until browned. Remove patties from skillet. Add mushrooms and onion to skillet, and sauté 6 minutes or until tender. Stir in prepared gravy, and bring to a light boil. Return patties to skillet, and spoon gravy over each patty. Cover, reduce heat to low, and simmer 8 to 10 minutes.

note: To make ahead, proceed with Step 1 as directed. Wrap each patty individually in plastic wrap, and place in a large zip-top plastic freezer bag. Freeze for up to 3 months. Thaw frozen patties in refrigerator 8 hours; proceed with Steps 2 and 3.

Gone Fishin'

Daddy's the reason I hate to fish. As a small child, he ruined it for me—despite his best intentions to the contrary. Early on a Saturday morning, he would ask, with great enthusiasm, "Wanna go fishin'?!" And I would get all excited, thinking about dipping my cork in the water and riding my bike around the lake and maybe scoring a boat ride somewhere in the mix. Then I would wait. And wait. For hours. By the time Daddy finally got his tackle box all arranged and his rods and reels adjusted an ice chest full of "Co-Colas" loaded into the pickup, I had lost all interest in catching fish. But eating them? Now that's something I can always get excited about. My mother's fried catfish—light, golden, and crispy—is the best you will ever taste, so let's not waste time arguing about that. If I close my eyes, I can hear my fork crunching into one of her fillets right now. And if you want a truly heavenly dining experience, pair that catfish with her coleslaw and puffy-as-air hush puppies. (In a shocking break with cast-iron tradition, she fries them in a Le Creuset Dutch oven.) Still, while I insist Mama is the Catfish Queen, I'm willing to entertain nominations for first runner-up. But she had better be good. Mama has set the bar pretty high.

VFL

Nashville-style hot catfish

makes: 6 to 8 servings   hands-on time: 45 min.
total time: 45 min., plus 1 day for chilling

½ cup buttermilk
1 (5-oz.) bottle habanero
   hot sauce
3 lb. small catfish fillets
2 cups all-purpose flour

2 tsp. salt
¾ tsp. pepper
¾ tsp. onion powder
   Vegetable oil
   Salt to taste

1. Whisk together buttermilk and hot sauce in a large bowl. Add catfish. Cover and chill 24 hours.

2. Combine flour and next 3 ingredients. Remove catfish from buttermilk mixture, discarding mixture. Dredge catfish in flour mixture, shaking off excess.

3. Pour oil to depth of 1½ inches into a large, deep skillet; heat to 325°. Fry catfish, in batches, 4 to 5 minutes on each side or until golden brown and fish flakes with a fork. Drain on a wire rack over paper towels. Sprinkle with salt to taste. Serve with additional hot sauce, if desired.

note: We tested with Tabasco Habanero Sauce.

Try This Twist!

Nashville-style hot chicken: Substitute 3 lb. chicken drumsticks for catfish. Proceed with recipe as directed through Step 2. Preheat oven to 350°. Pour oil to depth of 1 inch into a large, deep skillet; heat to 325°. Fry drumsticks, in batches, 6 to 8 minutes or until lightly browned, turning occasionally. Transfer to a wire rack in a jelly-roll pan. Bake 15 minutes or until done. hands-on time: 40 min.; total time: 55 min., plus 1 day for chilling.

classic Southern dishes

brown sugar-cinnamon peach pie

makes: 8 servings
hands-on time: 30 min.   total time: 4 hr., 50 min.

1⅓ cups cold butter
4¼ cups all-purpose flour, divided
1½ tsp. salt
½ to ¾ cup ice-cold water
8 large fresh, firm, ripe peaches (about 4 lb.)
½ cup firmly packed light brown sugar
⅓ cup granulated sugar
1 tsp. ground cinnamon
⅛ tsp. salt
1½ Tbsp. butter, cut into pieces
1 large egg, beaten
1½ Tbsp. granulated sugar

1. Cut 1⅓ cups butter into small cubes, and chill 15 minutes. Stir together 4 cups flour and 1½ tsp. salt. Cut butter into flour mixture with a pastry blender until mixture resembles small peas. Gradually stir in ½ cup ice water with a fork, stirring until dry ingredients are moistened and dough begins to form a ball and leaves sides of bowl, adding more ice water, 1 Tbsp. at a time, if necessary. Turn dough out onto a piece of plastic wrap; press and shape dough into 2 flat disks. Wrap each disk in plastic wrap, and chill 30 minutes to 24 hours.

2. Preheat oven to 425°. Place 1 dough disk on a lightly floured surface; sprinkle dough lightly with flour. Roll dough to about ¼-inch thickness. Starting at 1 edge of dough, wrap dough around a rolling pin. Place rolling pin over a 9-inch pie plate, and unroll dough over pie plate. Press dough into pie plate.

3. Roll remaining dough disk to about ¼-inch thickness on a lightly floured surface. Cut into 3 (1½-inch-wide) strips and 8 (¼-inch-wide) strips using a fluted pastry wheel.

4. Peel peaches, and cut into ½-inch-thick slices; cut slices in half. Stir together brown sugar, next 3 ingredients, and remaining ¼ cup flour in a bowl; add peaches, stirring to coat. Immediately spoon peach mixture into piecrust in pie plate, and dot with 1½ Tbsp. butter. (Do not make mixture ahead or it will become too juicy.)

5. Carefully place dough strips over filling, making a lattice design. Crimp edges of pie. Brush lattice with beaten egg; sprinkle with 1½ Tbsp. granulated sugar.

6. Freeze pie 15 minutes. Meanwhile, heat a jelly-roll pan in oven 10 minutes. Place pie on hot jelly-roll pan.

7. Bake at 425° on lower oven rack 15 minutes. Reduce oven temperature to 375°; bake 40 minutes. Cover loosely with aluminum foil to prevent excessive browning, and bake 25 more minutes or until juices are thick and bubbly (juices will bubble through top). Transfer to a wire rack; cool 2 hours before serving.

lime-cornmeal cookies (pictured on opposite page, back left)

makes: about 2½ dozen
hands-on time: 20 min.   total time: 10 hr.

1¼ cups all-purpose flour
½   cup plain yellow cornmeal
½   cup butter, softened
½   cup sugar
1   large egg
1   Tbsp. lime zest
1   Tbsp. fresh lime juice
½   tsp. vanilla extract
Wax paper

1. Combine flour and cornmeal. Beat butter and sugar at medium speed with an electric mixer until light and fluffy. Add egg and next 3 ingredients, beating until blended. Gradually add flour mixture, beating just until blended after each addition. Cover and chill dough 1 hour. Shape dough into a 12-inch log using wax paper. Wrap tightly in plastic wrap, and chill 8 hours.

2. Preheat oven to 375°. Cut log into ¼-inch-thick slices. Place 1 inch apart on ungreased baking sheets. Bake 12 minutes or until set. Transfer to wire racks; cool completely (about 15 minutes).

Try This Twist!

◊ **chocolate-orange cornmeal cookies:** (pictured on opposite page, back right) Substitute orange zest and fresh orange juice for lime zest and juice. Drizzle ¼ cup melted semisweet chocolate morsels over cooled cookies.

bacon-peanut truffles (pictured on opposite page, front right)

makes: about 2 dozen
hands-on time: 30 min.   total time: 4 hr.

2   Tbsp. dark brown sugar
¼   tsp. salt
¾   cup honey-roasted peanuts
8   thick bacon slices, cooked and divided
⅓   cup creamy peanut butter
Parchment paper
6   oz. bittersweet chocolate, chopped

1. Process first 3 ingredients and 6 bacon slices in a food processor 20 to 30 seconds or until finely ground. Stir together bacon mixture and peanut butter in a small bowl until smooth. Cover and chill 2 hours.

2. Shape rounded teaspoonfuls of bacon mixture into ¾-inch balls. Place on a parchment paper-lined baking sheet; chill 1 hour.

3. Chop remaining 2 bacon slices. Microwave chocolate in a microwave-safe bowl at HIGH 1 to 1½ minutes or until melted and smooth, stirring at 30-second intervals. Dip chilled bacon balls into chocolate. Place on a parchment paper-lined baking sheet. Immediately sprinkle tops with chopped bacon. Chill 30 minutes before serving. Store in an airtight container in refrigerator for up to 2 weeks.

classic Southern dishes

83

GRACIOUS

entertaining

strawberry margarita spritzers

(pictured on opposite page, front right)

makes: about 8 cups
hands-on time: 10 min.   total time: 10 min.

1 (10-oz.) package frozen whole strawberries, thawed
1 (10-oz.) can frozen straw-berry daiquiri mix, thawed
1 cup tequila
¼ cup orange liqueur
2 Tbsp. fresh lime juice
1 (1-liter) bottle club soda, chilled
Garnish: halved fresh strawberries

1. Pulse first 5 ingredients in a blender until smooth. Pour into a pitcher, and stir in club soda just before serving. Serve over ice. Garnish, if desired.

note: We tested with Triple Sec orange liqueur.

beer 'garitas (pictured on opposite page, back)

For fast measuring, you can use the empty can of limeade concentrate to measure the tequila. One 12-oz. can is equivalent to 1½ cups. Serve in salt-rimmed glasses, if desired.

makes: about 6 cups   hands-on time: 5 min.   total time: 5 min.

1 (12-oz.) container limeade concentrate, thawed
1½ cups tequila
2 (12-oz.) bottles beer
Crushed ice
Garnish: lime wedges

1. Stir together first 3 ingredients in a large pitcher until blended. Serve immediately over crushed ice. Garnish, if desired.

note: We tested with Yazoo Dos Perros Ale, Grolsch Premium Lager, Truck Stop Honey Brown Ale, and Bud Light beer.

loaded baked potato dip

(pictured on opposite page, front right)

Waffle fries make great dippers for this dip. We baked them extra-crispy.

makes: about 4 cups
hands-on time: 15 min.   total time: 1 hr., 25 min.

1 (2.1-oz.) package fully cooked
   bacon slices
1 (16-oz.) container sour cream
2 cups (8 oz.) freshly shredded
   sharp Cheddar cheese
⅓ cup sliced fresh chives
2 tsp. hot sauce
Garnishes: cooked, crumbled
   bacon; sliced fresh chives

1. Microwave bacon according to package directions until crisp; drain on paper towels. Cool 10 minutes; crumble. Stir together bacon and next 4 ingredients. Cover and chill 1 to 24 hours before serving. Garnish, if desired. Serve with crispy, warm waffle fries. Store leftovers in refrigerator up to 7 days. Just before serving, garnish, if desired.

note: We tested with Oscar Mayer Fully Cooked Bacon.

warm artichoke-shrimp dip

(pictured on opposite page, back left)

Serve this rich dip with pita chips and breadsticks.

makes: about 4 cups
hands-on time: 15 min.   total time: 15 min.

2 (14-oz.) cans artichoke hearts,
   drained and chopped
1 cup freshly grated Parmesan
   cheese
¾ cup mayonnaise
½ cup fine, dry breadcrumbs
2 garlic cloves, minced
2 Tbsp. lemon juice
½ lb. peeled, cooked shrimp,
   chopped
Garnishes: lemon zest,
   chopped fresh parsley

1. Combine artichoke hearts and next 5 ingredients in a large saucepan. Cook over medium heat, stirring often, 4 to 5 minutes or until thoroughly heated. Stir in shrimp. Transfer to a serving bowl. Garnish, if desired.

entertaining

The Secret Ingredient

One great joy of my marriage has been introducing my Midwestern husband to Southern food. The fried green tomato was a revelation to him. Ditto gumbo, banana pudding, and Mama's fried chicken. His favorite discovery has to be the muffuletta, an olive-laced delight served on crunchy-flaky bread all along the Louisiana and Mississippi Gulf Coasts. (Insiders tell us the bread often comes from Gambino's bakery in New Orleans.) While my husband hasn't yet made it to Central Grocery in "NOLA," supposedly the birthplace of muffulettas, the two of us have sampled them at two of our favorite Mississippi haunts: the Government Street Grocery in Ocean Springs and Trapani's Eatery in Bay St. Louis. Over the years, we've struggled, in vain, to determine which one is the best. Finally, we gave up and decided to just hit both spots on every trip. Through trial and error, I've learned to make a muffuletta knockoff at home in Birmingham. The flavor's good, but the bread's not quite right, and there's a crucial ingredient missing—the Gulf. This fine sandwich just doesn't taste the same unless you can smell salt air from your table. Still, if you can't get to the coast anytime soon, break out the olive salad, and give it a try.

VFL

muffuletta dip

Serve this versatile recipe over a block of cream cheese along with crackers, or toss it with leftovers in a Caesar salad. Parmesan cheese helps hold the ingredients together.

makes: about 4 cups
hands-on time: 10 min.　　total time: 1 hr., 10 min.

1　cup Italian olive salad, drained	1　(2¼-oz.) can sliced black olives, drained
1　cup diced salami (about 4 oz.)	4　oz. provolone cheese, diced
¼　cup grated Parmesan cheese	1　celery rib, finely chopped
¼　cup chopped pepperoncini salad peppers	½　red bell pepper, chopped
	1　Tbsp. olive oil
	¼　cup chopped fresh parsley

1. Stir together first 9 ingredients. Cover and chill 1 to 24 hours before serving. Stir in parsley just before serving. Serve with French bread crostini. Store leftovers in refrigerator for up to 5 days.

note: We tested with Boscoli Italian Olive Salad.

Y'ALL ENJOY

Cinco de Mayo

10 servings

Spicy Queso Dip   **Fresh Salsa**

Easy Barbecue Tostadas *(page 118)*   **Oven-Baked Churros** *(page 127)*

fresh salsa (pictured on opposite page, top left)

makes: about 4 cups
hands-on time: 15 min.   total time: 15 min.

¼   medium-size sweet onion
1   small garlic clove, quartered
1   jalapeño pepper, seeded and
    quartered
¼   cup loosely packed fresh
    cilantro leaves
2   lb. tomatoes
1   lime
1¼ tsp. salt

1. Coarsely chop onion. Pulse onion and next 3 ingredients in a food processor until finely chopped.

2. Cut each tomato into 4 pieces. Cut core from each piece; discard core. Add tomatoes to food processor in batches, and pulse each batch until well blended. Transfer to a large bowl. Squeeze juice from lime over salsa, and stir in salt. Serve with cut vegetables and pita chips.

spicy queso dip (pictured on opposite page, bottom right)

makes: about 3 cups
hands-on time: 20 min.   total time: 20 min.

1   small onion, diced
1   Tbsp. oil
1   garlic clove, minced
1   (16-oz.) package pepper Jack
    pasteurized prepared cheese
    product, cubed
1   (10-oz.) can diced tomatoes
    and green chiles
2   Tbsp. chopped fresh cilantro

1. Cook onion in hot oil in a large nonstick skillet over medium-high heat 8 minutes or until tender. Add garlic, and cook 1 minute. Remove from heat.

2. Combine cheese, tomatoes, and onion mixture in a large microwave-safe glass bowl. Microwave at HIGH 5 minutes, stirring every 2½ minutes. Stir in cilantro. Serve with tortilla chips.

note: We tested with Velveeta Pepper Jack.

gracious

92

green goddess dip

Serve this dip with blanched green or white asparagus spears, sliced cauliflower florets, halved baby zucchini, blanched sugar snap peas, blanched haricots verts (tiny green beans).

makes: about 1⅔ cups
hands-on time: 15 min.   total time: 2 hr., 15 min.

¾ cup mayonnaise
¾ cup sour cream
½ cup loosely packed fresh
     flat-leaf parsley leaves
1 Tbsp. chopped fresh tarragon
2 tsp. white wine vinegar
1 tsp. anchovy paste
1 tsp. lemon zest
1 Tbsp. fresh lemon juice
2 garlic cloves, minced
⅓ cup chopped fresh chives
Salt and freshly ground pepper
     to taste
Garnish: chopped fresh tarragon

1. Process first 9 ingredients in a food processor until smooth, stopping to scrape down sides if needed. Stir in chives; season with salt and pepper to taste. Cover and chill 2 to 24 hours. Garnish, if desired. Serve with assorted vegetables.

TASTE OF WINTER

LEMONS

Whether you use the juice, the zest (rind), or the slices, the acidity of lemons brightens the flavor in all types of food. Select lemons that have smooth, bright yellow skin (green means they are underripe) and feel heavy for their size. Store fresh lemons for 2 to 3 weeks in a zip-top plastic freezer bag in the refrigerator.

Y'ALL ENJOY

Appetizers Outdoors

8 to 10 servings

Green Goddess Dip *(page 95)*

Bacon-Parmesan Tassies

Shrimp Salad-Stuffed Endive *(page 98)*   Summer Fruit Salad *(page 111)*

Chicken-and-Tortellini Salad *(page 111)*

Sweet Pea Crostini *(page 98)*

Gorgonzola-Grilled Pear Crostini *(page 99)*

bacon-parmesan tassies (pictured on opposite page, top left)

makes: 2 dozen   hands-on time: 30 min.   total time: 2 hr.

½   cup butter, softened

½   (8-oz.) package cream
      cheese, softened

1¼ cups all-purpose flour

½   cup half-and-half

1   large egg

⅛   tsp. salt

4   bacon slices, cooked and
      crumbled

½   cup grated Parmesan cheese

¼   cup chopped fresh chives

1. Beat butter and cream cheese at medium speed with an electric mixer until creamy. Gradually add flour to butter mixture, beating at low speed until blended. Shape mixture into 24 balls, and place on a baking sheet; cover and chill 1 hour.

2. Place dough balls into cups of a lightly greased 24-cup miniature muffin pan; press dough, forming a shell.

3. Preheat oven to 375°. Whisk together half-and-half and next 2 ingredients. Sprinkle bacon into pastry shells; top each with 1 tsp. cheese. Drizzle half-and-half mixture over cheese. Sprinkle chives over half-and-half mixture.

4. Bake at 375° for 25 to 30 minutes or until puffed and golden brown. Remove from pan to a wire rack, and cool 5 minutes. Serve warm.

gracious

96

sweet pea crostini (pictured at right)

makes: 20 appetizer servings   **hands-on time: 15 min.**
total time: 2 hr., 15 min.

2	(9-oz.) packages frozen sweet peas, thawed
3	garlic cloves, chopped
3	Tbsp. extra virgin olive oil
2	Tbsp. fresh lemon juice

Salt and freshly ground pepper to taste
40 French bread baguette slices, toasted
½ cup (2 oz.) crumbled blue cheese or goat cheese

1. Place peas and garlic in a food processor; with processor running, pour oil through food chute in a slow, steady stream, processing until smooth. Stir in lemon juice; season with salt and pepper to taste. Cover and chill 2 hours.

2. Spoon pea mixture onto toasted baguette slices; sprinkle with cheese.

shrimp salad-stuffed endive

makes: 24 appetizer servings   **hands-on time: 20 min.**
total time: 20 min.

¼ cup mayonnaise
¼ cup cream cheese, softened
2 Tbsp. finely chopped green onions
1 Tbsp. finely chopped fresh parsley
1 tsp. lemon zest
1 Tbsp. fresh lemon juice

1 garlic clove, pressed
¼ tsp. salt
¼ tsp. ground red pepper
2½ cups finely chopped, peeled and deveined, cooked shrimp (about 1 lb. of any size)
½ cup finely diced celery
24 Belgian endive leaves

1. Stir together mayonnaise, cream cheese, and next 7 ingredients in a large bowl; stir in finely chopped shrimp and finely diced celery.

2. Spoon shrimp mixture onto bottom half of endive leaves. Serve immediately.

gorgonzola-grilled pear crostini (pictured on page 97, bottom right)

makes: 36 crostini
hands-on time: 22 min.   total time: 22 min.

3 firm, ripe Bartlett pears, cut into ¼-inch-thick wedges
½ (8-oz.) package cream cheese, softened
4 oz. Gorgonzola cheese, crumbled
¼ cup butter, softened
2 Tbsp. dry sherry

36 French bread baguette slices, toasted
½ cup finely chopped, lightly salted roasted pecans
2 Tbsp. finely chopped fresh rosemary
¼ cup honey

1. Preheat grill to 350° to 400° (medium-high) heat. Grill pear wedges, covered with grill lid, 1 to 2 minutes on each side or until golden.

2. Stir together cream cheese and next 3 ingredients; spread about ½ Tbsp. on each baguette slice. Top with grilled pears; sprinkle with pecans and rosemary, and drizzle with honey.

Covered-Dish Special

Deviled eggs are trickier than they look. Boil the eggs too long, and they turn an unappealing shade of avocado; take them out too soon, and you've got deviled eggs over easy. Too much mayo turns them into, well, yellow mayo, while too little makes them so dry that even your preacher won't be able to force one down at the church social, just to be nice. And yet, for generations, Southern cooks from Richmond to El Paso have persevered. Why? Because good deviled eggs are well worth the effort. They sort of punctuate your dinner plate, especially if you get all artistic with them. My life changed when a foodie friend taught me to spoon the egg mixture into a plastic bag, snip off one corner, and then pipe the mixture back into the halved egg whites. At that moment, I became worthy of a spot on the church hostess committee. Deviled eggs are important, plain and simple. Without them, fellowship halls across the South would have to close their doors, paprika demand would plummet, and there could be no more ladies' luncheons. (We can't expect cucumber sandwiches and crab dip to carry the burden alone.) But there's a larger, much more important issue at stake: We need that deviled egg plate as a fallback shower gift for the bride-to-be who has everything.

VFL

deviled eggs with assorted toppings

The filling for Southern-style basic deviled eggs is nothing more than egg yolks, mayonnaise, hot sauce, and green onion. The festive toppings make these deviled eggs perfect for potlucks, tailgates, and summer suppers.

makes: 8 servings
hands-on time: 15 min.   **total time: 15 min.**

1   dozen hard-cooked eggs, peeled
½   cup mayonnaise
1   green onion, finely chopped
2   tsp. hot sauce
Salt and freshly ground pepper to taste

Toppings: chopped cooked bacon, smoked salmon, chopped black olives, chopped Spanish olives, sour cream, chopped sun-dried tomatoes, and chopped fresh herbs (dill, parsley, chives)

1. Slice eggs in half lengthwise, and carefully remove yolks. Reserve egg whites.

2. Mash yolks with mayonnaise, onion, and hot sauce until well blended. Season with salt and pepper to taste. Spoon or pipe yolk mixture into reserved egg whites. Serve immediately, or cover and chill for up to 1 day. Serve with desired toppings.

grilled jalapeño-lime corn on the cob

Add south-of-the-border flavor to buttery grilled corn with jalapeño peppers, cilantro, and lime juice.

makes: 8 servings   hands-on time: 30 min.   total time: 30 min.

8   ears fresh corn, husks
    removed
Vegetable cooking spray
Salt and freshly ground pepper
    to taste
½   cup butter, softened
1   jalapeño pepper, seeded and
    minced
1   small garlic clove, pressed
1   Tbsp. lime zest
1   Tbsp. fresh lime juice
2   tsp. chopped fresh cilantro

1. Preheat grill to 350° to 400° (medium-high) heat. Coat corn lightly with cooking spray. Sprinkle with desired amount of salt and pepper. Grill corn, covered with grill lid, 15 minutes or until golden brown, turning occasionally.

2. Meanwhile, stir together butter and next 5 ingredients. Remove corn from grill, and cut into thirds. Serve corn with butter mixture.

TASTE OF SUMMER

CORN

Whether served hot off the grill or mixed in salads or casseroles, fresh-picked corn boasts a sweet flavor. May through September is peak season. A fresh husk is the number one thing to look for. Deep brown silk tips or ends mean it's ripe, but the whole silk shouldn't be dried up. Open the tip of the husk to see if the kernels are all the way to the end of the ear; kernels should be plump when pinched.

hot bacon potato salad with green beans

Classic potato salad ingredients get a twist from bacon and green beans. We love this paired with a perfectly grilled steak.

makes: 8 servings   hands-on time: 30 min.   total time: 30 min.

3   lb. fingerling potatoes, cut in half
1   (8-oz.) package haricots verts (tiny green beans)
½   cup white wine vinegar
1   shallot, minced
3   Tbsp. honey
1   Tbsp. Dijon mustard
1½   tsp. salt
1   tsp. pepper
½   cup olive oil
2   Tbsp. chopped fresh dill
¼   cup coarsely chopped fresh parsley
4   fully cooked bacon slices, chopped

1. Bring potatoes and water to cover to a boil in a large Dutch oven over medium-high heat, and cook 20 minutes or until tender. Drain.

2. Meanwhile, cook green beans in boiling water to cover in a medium saucepan 3 to 4 minutes or until crisp-tender. Plunge into ice water to stop the cooking process; drain.

3. Whisk together vinegar and next 5 ingredients in a medium bowl. Add oil in a slow, steady stream, whisking constantly, until smooth.

4. Pour vinegar mixture over potatoes. Just before serving, add green beans, dill, and parsley, and toss gently until blended. Sprinkle with bacon. Serve immediately, or cover and chill until ready to serve.

grilled green tomatoes caprese

(pictured on opposite page, back)

makes: 8 to 10 servings
hands-on time: 21 min.   total time: 1 hr., 21 min.

½   cup olive oil
¼   cup white balsamic vinegar
2   garlic cloves, minced
1   Tbsp. brown sugar
⅛   tsp. salt
4   medium-size green tomatoes,
    cut into ¼-inch-thick slices
    (about 2 lb.)
1   (16-oz.) package sliced fresh
    mozzarella cheese
Kosher salt and freshly ground
    pepper to taste
⅓   cup thinly sliced fresh basil

1. Combine first 5 ingredients in a large zip-top plastic freezer bag; add tomatoes, seal, and shake gently to coat. Chill 1 hour.

2. Preheat grill to 350° to 400° (medium-high) heat. Remove tomatoes from marinade, reserving marinade. Grill tomatoes, covered with grill lid, 3 to 4 minutes on each side or until tender and grill marks appear.

3. Arrange alternating slices of warm grilled tomatoes and mozzarella cheese on a large, shallow platter. Drizzle with reserved marinade; season with salt and pepper to taste. Sprinkle with basil.

simple grilled asparagus

(pictured on opposite page, front)

makes: 8 servings   hands-on time: 14 min.   total time: 14 min.

Vegetable cooking spray
1½ lb. fresh asparagus
1   Tbsp. extra virgin olive oil
½   tsp. kosher salt, divided
¼   tsp. freshly ground pepper
½   lemon
¼   cup shaved Parmesan cheese

1. Coat cold cooking grate of grill with cooking spray, and place on grill. Preheat grill to 350° to 400° (medium-high) heat. Snap off, and discard tough ends of asparagus.

2. Place asparagus in a shallow dish; add oil and ¼ tsp. salt, and toss well to coat. Grill asparagus 2 minutes on each side or until crisp-tender.

3. Add pepper and remaining ¼ tsp. salt. Squeeze juice from lemon over asparagus; sprinkle with cheese.

grilled peppers and mushrooms

makes: 8 servings hands-on time: 20 min. total time: 50 min.

¼ cup white balsamic vinegar*
2 Tbsp. coarse-grained Dijon mustard
1 Tbsp. honey
½ tsp. salt
¼ tsp. coarsely ground pepper
½ cup olive oil
4 large assorted bell peppers, cut into 2-inch-wide strips
1 large red onion, thickly sliced
1 (8-oz.) package baby portobello mushrooms
Salt and freshly ground pepper to taste
Garnish: fresh rosemary

1. Whisk together first 5 ingredients. Gradually add oil in a slow, steady stream, whisking constantly until blended. Reserve 2 Tbsp. mixture; cover and chill. Stir bell peppers and next 2 ingredients into remaining vinegar mixture. Cover and chill 30 minutes.

2. Preheat grill to 350° to 400° (medium-high) heat. Remove vegetables from vinegar mixture; discard mixture. Grill vegetables at the same time, placing peppers, skin side down, on cooking grate. Grill vegetables, covered with grill lid, 6 minutes or until peppers look blistered and grill marks appear. Turn vegetables, and grill about 2 more minutes or until crisp-tender.

3. Arrange vegetables in a single layer on a serving platter. Drizzle with reserved 2 Tbsp. vinegar mixture just before serving. Season with salt and pepper to taste. Garnish, if desired.

*White wine vinegar may be substituted.

note: Prep the vinaigrette 3 days ahead; wash and cut the peppers 1 day ahead.

TASTE OF SUMMER

BELL PEPPERS

Bell peppers are at their best from July through September. Look for firm, nicely colored fruit that is fragrant at the stem end. Avoid peppers that are damp, because they can mold. Store them in a plastic bag in the refrigerator for up to a week. They can also be sliced or chopped and frozen in a freezer bag up to 6 months. Be sure to wash peppers just before using them.

summer fruit salad (pictured on opposite page, back left)

makes: 8 to 10 appetizer servings
hands-on time: 20 min.   total time: 20 min.

½ cup bottled poppy seed
  dressing
2 tsp. grated fresh ginger
2 avocados, thinly sliced
4 cups loosely packed arugula
2 cups halved seedless red
  grapes
1 mango, julienned
1 cup diced fresh strawberries
¼ cup thinly sliced green onions
¼ cup chopped fresh cilantro

1. Whisk together dressing and grated ginger in a large bowl. Cut avocado slices in half crosswise; gently toss with dressing mixture. Add arugula and remaining ingredients; gently toss to coat. Serve immediately.

chicken-and-tortellini salad

(pictured on opposite page, front right)

makes: 12 to 15 appetizer servings
hands-on time: 20 min.   total time: 30 min.

2 (9-oz.) packages refrigerated
  cheese-filled tortellini
½ cup olive oil
½ cup grated Parmesan cheese
¼ cup fresh lemon juice
2 garlic cloves
1 tsp. Worcestershire sauce
2 cups chopped cooked chicken
1 cup frozen sweet peas, thawed
½ cup thinly sliced green onions
½ cup chopped fresh flat-leaf
  parsley
Salt and pepper to taste

1. Prepare tortellini according to package directions.

2. Process olive oil and next 4 ingredients in a blender until smooth. Toss olive oil mixture with tortellini, chicken, and next 3 ingredients. Season with salt and pepper to taste.

Y'ALL ENJOY

Spring Brunch

4 to 6 servings

Fried Chicken Bites

Fruit, Cheese, and Herb Skewers

Strawberry-Rhubarb Hand Pies (*page 115*)

---

fried chicken bites (pictured on opposite page, top left)

makes: 4 to 6 servings
hands-on time: 50 min.
total time: 50 min., plus 1 day for marinating

1½ tsp. to 1 Tbsp. ground
    red pepper
1½ tsp. ground chipotle
    chile pepper
1½ tsp. garlic powder
1½ tsp. dried crushed red pepper
1½ tsp. ground black pepper
¾ tsp. salt
½ tsp. paprika
2 lb. skinned and boned
    chicken breasts
2 cups buttermilk
3 bread slices, toasted
1 cup all-purpose flour
Peanut oil
Salt to taste
Blue cheese dressing or
    honey mustard

1. Combine first 7 ingredients; reserve half of spice mixture. Cut chicken into 1-inch pieces. Place chicken in a medium bowl; toss with remaining spice mixture until coated. Stir in buttermilk; cover and chill 24 hours. Tear bread into pieces; place in a food processor with reserved spice mixture. Process until mixture resembles cornmeal. Stir in flour. Remove chicken from buttermilk. Dredge chicken in breadcrumb mixture.

2. Pour oil to depth of 2 inches into a Dutch oven; heat to 350°. Fry chicken, in batches, 6 to 7 minutes on each side or until golden brown and done. Drain on a wire rack over paper towels. Sprinkle with salt to taste. Serve warm or cold with blue cheese dressing or honey mustard.

fruit, cheese, and herb skewers

Thread various combinations of fruit, fresh small mozzarella cheese balls, and herbs on 6-inch wooden skewers up to 3 hours ahead.

◇ **blackberry skewers:** 2 basil leaves, 2 fresh small mozzarella cheese balls, 2 to 3 blackberries (pictured on opposite page, bottom right)

◇ **raspberry skewers:** 2 mint leaves, 2 fresh small mozzarella cheese balls, 4 raspberries

strawberry-rhubarb hand pies

Crisp rhubarb has a tart flavor that teams perfectly with sweet strawberries.

makes: 2 dozen   hands-on time: 1 hr.   total time: 2 hr., 10 min.

¾ cup finely diced fresh strawberries

¾ cup finely diced rhubarb

1 Tbsp. cornstarch

6 Tbsp. sugar, divided

3 tsp. orange zest, divided

2¼ cups all-purpose flour

¼ tsp. salt

½ cup butter, cold

¼ cup shortening, chilled

3 Tbsp. ice-cold water

3 Tbsp. orange juice

Parchment paper

1 egg yolk, beaten

1 Tbsp. whipping cream

Sugar

1. Combine strawberries, rhubarb, cornstarch, 2 Tbsp. sugar, and 1½ tsp. orange zest in a small bowl.

2. Preheat oven to 375°. Combine flour, salt, and remaining ¼ cup sugar in a large bowl. Cut in butter and shortening with a pastry blender until mixture resembles small peas. Stir in remaining 1½ tsp. orange zest. Drizzle with ice-cold water and orange juice. Stir with a fork until combined. (Mixture will be crumbly and dry.) Knead mixture lightly, and shape dough into a disk. Divide dough in half.

3. Roll half of dough to ⅛-inch thickness on a heavily floured surface. (Cover remaining dough with plastic wrap.) Cut with a 2¼-inch round cutter, rerolling scraps as needed. Place half of dough rounds 2 inches apart on parchment paper-lined baking sheets. Top with 1 rounded teaspoonful strawberry mixture. Dampen edges of dough with water, and top with remaining dough rounds, pressing edges to seal. Crimp edges with a fork, and cut a slit in top of each round for steam to escape. Repeat procedure with remaining dough and strawberry mixture.

4. Stir together egg yolk and cream; brush pies with egg wash. Sprinkle with sugar. Freeze pies 10 minutes.

5. Bake at 375° for 20 to 25 minutes or until lightly browned. Cool 10 minutes. Serve warm or at room temperature. Store in an airtight container for up to 2 days.

WINTER SQUASH

Acorn, butternut, spaghetti, and other winter squash are picked in the autumn and stored until spring. For the best taste, choose squash that are full, firm, and heavy, and that feel "corky" when you press them gently. Look for ones with skins that have a deep color with a matte finish. Avoid squash with cracks, soft spots, and moldy areas. You don't have to refrigerate squash; keep it in a paper bag in a cool, dark place for up to a month. Don't store winter squash in plastic bags for more than 3 days because the plastic traps moisture, which can cause the squash to rot.

butternut squash spoon bread

For the ideal texture, we recommend serving this immediately once baked.

makes: 8 servings
hands-on time: 25 min.   total time: 1 hr., 10 min.

2 cups buttermilk	1 tsp. baking powder
4 large eggs, separated	1 tsp. chopped fresh
2 cups thawed, frozen	rosemary
unseasoned, pureed	$\frac{1}{2}$ tsp. baking soda
butternut squash	$\frac{1}{2}$ tsp. salt
$\frac{1}{3}$ cup freshly grated	$\frac{1}{4}$ cup butter, melted
Parmesan cheese	
1 cup stone-ground white	
cornmeal	

1. Preheat oven to 350°. Cook buttermilk in a heavy saucepan over medium-high heat, stirring often, 4 to 6 minutes or until bubbles appear around edges (do not boil); remove from heat. (Mixture may curdle.)

2. Lightly beat egg yolks in a large bowl; stir in squash and cheese. Combine cornmeal and next 4 ingredients in a small bowl. Stir cornmeal mixture into squash mixture. Pour warm buttermilk over squash mixture; whisk until smooth. Let stand 15 minutes or until lukewarm.

3. Brush a 2½- to 3-qt. baking dish or 12-inch cast-iron skillet with 1 Tbsp. melted butter; stir remaining melted butter into squash mixture.

4. Beat egg whites at high speed with an electric mixer until stiff peaks form. Carefully fold into squash mixture. Pour mixture into prepared baking dish.

5. Bake at 350° for 30 to 35 minutes or until top is golden and a wooden pick inserted in center comes out clean.

note: We tested with Birds Eye Southland Butternut Squash. Buy 2 (12-oz.) packages to measure 2 cups.

entertaining

117

easy barbecue tostadas

Pick up shredded pork or chicken from your favorite barbecue place. The barbecue sauce can be made up to two days ahead.

makes: 10 servings   hands-on time: 10 min.   total time: 30 min.

10 tostada shells
1   (16-oz.) can refried beans
2   lb. shredded barbecued
    pork or chicken without sauce
Mole Barbecue Sauce
Chipotle Sour Cream
Jicama Slaw

1. Spread tostada shells with refried beans. Top with barbecued pork or chicken, Mole Barbecue Sauce, Chipotle Sour Cream, and Jicama Slaw. Serve immediately.

Mole Barbecue Sauce: Dissolve 1 Tbsp. mole sauce in ¼ cup hot water, whisking until smooth. Whisk in 1 cup barbecue sauce, 1 Tbsp. lime juice, and 1 Tbsp. chopped fresh cilantro. makes: about 1 ½ cups. hands-on time: 5 min., total time: 5 min.

Chipotle Sour Cream: Stir together ½ cup sour cream; 1 chipotle pepper in adobo sauce, minced; and a pinch of salt. makes: ½ cup. hands-on time: 5 min., total time: 5 min.

jicama slaw

makes: 10 servings   hands-on time: 10 min.   total time: 10 min.

2   cups shredded red cabbage
    (about ½ medium-size red
    cabbage)
2   cups thinly sliced jicama (about
    ½ medium jicama)
¼   cup thinly sliced red onion
¼   cup chopped fresh cilantro
1   Tbsp. olive oil
1   Tbsp. fresh lime juice
½   tsp. salt
½   tsp. sugar

1. Toss together all ingredients.

Y'ALL ENJOY

Dockside Celebration

8 servings

Smoky Chicken Barbecue Kabobs with White Barbecue Sauce

Deviled Eggs with Assorted Toppings (*page 101*)

Hot Bacon Potato Salad with Green Beans (*page 105*)

Grilled Jalapeño-Lime Corn on the Cob (*page 102*)

Fizzy, Fruity Ice-Cream Floats (*page 127*)

smoky chicken barbecue kabobs

(pictured on opposite page, top left)

makes: 8 servings
hands-on time: 20 min.
total time: 30 min., including rub and sauce

2   lb. skinned and boned
    chicken breasts
½   large red onion, cut into
    fourths and separated into
    pieces
1   pt. cherry tomatoes
8   (8-inch) metal skewers
Smoky Barbecue Rub
White Barbecue Sauce

1. Preheat grill to 350° to 400° (medium-high) heat. Cut chicken into 1-inch cubes. Thread chicken, onion, and tomatoes alternately onto skewers, leaving a ¼-inch space between pieces. Sprinkle kabobs with Smoky Barbecue Rub. Grill kabobs, covered with grill lid, 4 to 5 minutes on each side. Serve with White Barbecue Sauce.

Smoky Barbecue Rub: Stir together 2 Tbsp. firmly packed dark brown sugar, 2 tsp. garlic salt, 1 tsp. ground chipotle chile pepper, ½ tsp. ground cumin, and ¼ tsp. dried oregano.

White Barbecue Sauce: Stir together 1½ cups mayonnaise, ⅓ cup white vinegar, 1 tsp. coarsely ground pepper, ½ tsp. salt, ½ tsp. sugar, and 1 pressed garlic clove.

gracious

smoked paprika pork roast with sticky stout barbecue sauce

We "dry-brined" the pork before grilling it. This method calls for rubbing a mixture on the pork and chilling it, which allows the salt to pull the seasonings into the meat and improve juiciness and flavor. Unlike "wet" marinades, you chill the meat uncovered to keep the rub "dry."

makes: 8 servings
hands-on time: 25 min.   total time: 25 hr., 30 min.

2 Tbsp. smoked paprika
2 Tbsp. brown sugar
1 Tbsp. kosher salt
1 garlic clove, pressed
1 tsp. coarsely ground pepper
4 tsp. chopped fresh thyme, divided
1 (3½- to 4-lb.) boneless pork loin roast
Kitchen string
Sticky Stout Barbecue Sauce

1. Stir together first 5 ingredients and 2 tsp. thyme. Trim pork roast. Rub paprika mixture over pork. Tie roast with kitchen string at 1½-inch intervals, and place in a 13- x 9-inch baking dish. Chill, uncovered, 24 hours.

2. Light 1 side of grill, and preheat to 350° to 400° (medium-high) heat; leave other side unlit. Place pork over lit side, and grill, covered with lid, 8 minutes on each side or until browned. Transfer pork to unlit side, and grill, covered with lid, 35 to 45 minutes or until a meat thermometer inserted in thickest portion registers 145°. Let stand 10 minutes. Brush with Sticky Stout Barbecue Sauce. Sprinkle with remaining 2 tsp. thyme. Serve with remaining sauce.

sticky stout barbecue sauce

makes: about 2 cups
hands-on time: 25 min.   total time: 25 min.

1 small onion, finely chopped
1 Tbsp. vegetable oil
2 garlic cloves, minced
1 (11.2-oz.) bottle stout beer
1 cup spicy barbecue sauce
¼ cup fig preserves
2 Tbsp. cider vinegar

1. Sauté onion in hot oil in a large saucepan over medium-high heat 4 to 5 minutes or until tender. Add garlic; sauté 1 minute. Gradually stir in beer. Cook 8 to 10 minutes or until mixture is reduced by half. Reduce heat to medium.

2. Stir in barbecue sauce and next 2 ingredients, and cook 4 to 5 minutes or until thoroughly heated.

entertaining

caramelized pear cannoli with praline sauce

makes: 8 servings   hands-on time: 25 min.
total time: 3 hr., 35 min., including sauce

3   firm, ripe pears, cut into
    1-inch cubes
2   Tbsp. granulated sugar
1   Tbsp. butter, melted
Parchment paper
½   cup chopped pecans
1   (8-oz.) package mascarpone
    cheese
1   tsp. lemon zest
½   cup heavy cream
2   Tbsp. powdered sugar
8   (5-inch-long) cannoli shells
Praline Sauce

1. Preheat oven to 400°. Toss together first 3 ingredients. Spread in a single layer on a parchment paper-lined 15- x 10-inch jelly-roll pan. Bake at 400° for 30 to 35 minutes or until lightly browned and tender. Reduce oven temperature to 350°. Let pears cool 20 minutes.

2. Meanwhile, bake pecans at 350° in a single layer in a shallow pan 6 to 8 minutes or until toasted and fragrant, stirring halfway through.

3. Stir together pears, mascarpone, and lemon zest. Beat cream and powdered sugar at high speed with an electric mixer until soft peaks form. Fold whipped cream mixture into pear mixture.

4. Spoon pear mixture into a zip-top plastic freezer bag; snip 1 corner of bag to make a 1-inch hole. Pipe pear mixture into cannoli shells. Place in a 13- x 9-inch pan. Cover and chill 2 hours before serving. Serve cannoli with warm Praline Sauce, and sprinkle with toasted pecans.

note: We tested with cannoli shells purchased from our grocer's bakery. Ask the bakery clerk if you don't see them.

praline sauce

makes: about 2 cups
hands-on time: 10 min.   total time: 20 min.

1   cup firmly packed brown sugar
½   cup half-and-half
½   cup butter
½   tsp. vanilla extract

1. Bring first 3 ingredients to a boil in a small saucepan over medium heat, stirring constantly. Cook, stirring constantly, 1 minute. Remove from heat, and stir in vanilla; cool slightly (about 10 minutes).

PEARS

Pears are sweet and spicy, with a subtle, intoxicating perfume. And although a pear is usually thought of as fruit to be eaten in its natural state, it's actually as versatile as the apple, especially during its peak season. When selecting pears, test for ripeness by applying light thumb pressure near the pear's stem. If it's ripe, there will be a slight give. If the pears you've purchased aren't quite ripe, place them on a kitchen counter in a brown paper bag; check daily. It may take 3 to 5 days for them to fully ripen. Once ripe, store in the refrigerator for 3 to 5 days.

oven-baked churros (pictured on opposite page)

makes: 3 dozen   hands-on time: 15 min.   total time: 30 min.

1   (17.3-oz.) package frozen puff
     pastry sheets, thawed
Parchment paper
¼   cup sugar
1   tsp. ground cinnamon
¼   cup melted butter

1. Preheat oven to 450°. Unfold and cut puff pastry sheets in half lengthwise, and cut each half crosswise into 1-inch-wide strips. Place strips on a lightly greased parchment paper-lined baking sheet. Bake at 450° for 10 minutes or until golden brown.

2. Meanwhile, combine sugar and cinnamon. Remove pastry strips from oven, and dip in butter; roll in cinnamon-sugar mixture. Let stand on a wire rack 5 minutes or until dry.

iced Mexican chocolate sipper
(pictured on opposite page)

makes: about 7 cups
hands-on time: 10 min.   total time: 10 min.

2   (14-oz.) containers premium
     chocolate ice cream
2   cups milk
¾   to 1 tsp. ground cinnamon
½   tsp. orange zest
1   cup bourbon
Garnishes: orange zest curls,
     sweetened whipped cream,
     ground cinnamon

1. Pulse first 4 ingredients in a blender until smooth. Stir in bourbon. Serve immediately over ice. Garnish, if desired.

note: We tested with Häagen-Dazs Ice Cream.

fizzy, fruity ice-cream floats
(pictured on page 121, bottom right)

hands-on time: 5 min.   total time: 5 min.

Let guest pour their favorite fruit-flavored soft drinks (such as grape, lime, or cherry) over scoops of vanilla ice cream.

REFRESHED

bing cherry salad

Congealed salads are making a comeback at dinner parties across the South. This three-ingredient retro wonder is a delicious make-ahead addition to your menu and makes a pretty presentation in individual molds.

makes: 8 servings
hands-on time: 12 min.   total time: 9 hr., 50 min.

1   (15-oz.) can Bing cherries (dark, sweet pitted cherries)
2   (8-oz.) cans crushed pineapple in juice
1   (6-oz.) package cherry-flavored gelatin
1   cup cold water

1. Drain cherries and pineapple, reserving 1½ cups juice in a saucepan. (If necessary, add water to equal 1½ cups.) Bring juice mixture to a boil over medium heat; stir in gelatin, and cook, stirring constantly, 2 minutes or until gelatin dissolves. Remove from heat, and stir in 1 cup cold water. Chill until consistency of unbeaten egg whites (about 1½ hours).

2. Gently stir in drained cherries and pineapple. Pour mixture into an 8-inch square baking dish or 8 (⅔-cup) molds. Cover and chill 8 hours or until firm.

SIT A SPELL

Salad Secret

There's a case to be made for canned fruit. My mother used to serve something called "fruit cocktail" from a can. If memory serves, it had pears, cherries, pineapple, and some other tidbits I didn't recognize as a child. Having been raised on canned cranberry sauce, I didn't even like the real thing the first time I had it. It didn't jiggle enough, and it lacked the log-like solidity of the canned version. Mama's suppertime staple, though, was pear salad—canned pear halves with a dollop of mayo and shredded Cheddar cheese sprinkled on top. Like my mother, I go with pear salad when I can't think of anything else to fill out that supper plate. And on those nights when I can't dream up one more "fresh twist" on chicken, I break out the canned pineapple and stir-fry. Lesson learned: Before you buy any other kitchen tools, get yourself the Cadillac of can openers.

VFL

panzanella salad with cornbread croutons

Think cornbread salad with an Italian accent. A light, lemony vinaigrette replaces the traditional sour cream-and-mayo dressing.

makes: 6 to 8 servings
hands-on time: 25 min.
total time: 1 hr., 30 min., including cornbread

Skillet Cornbread,
    cooled completely
1 yellow bell pepper, diced
1 small red onion, diced
½ cup olive oil, divided
2 tsp. lemon zest
¼ cup fresh lemon juice
½ tsp. honey
Salt and freshly ground pepper
    to taste
1 pt. grape tomatoes, halved
½ English cucumber, quartered
    and sliced
½ cup pitted kalamata olives,
    halved
½ cup torn fresh basil leaves

1. Preheat oven to 400°. Cut cornbread into 1-inch cubes. Bake at 400° in a single layer on a lightly greased jelly-roll pan 15 minutes or until edges are golden, stirring halfway through.

2. Meanwhile, sauté bell pepper and onion in 1 Tbsp. hot olive oil in a small skillet over medium-high heat 5 minutes or until crisp-tender.

3. Whisk together lemon zest, lemon juice, honey, remaining 7 Tbsp. olive oil, and salt and pepper to taste in a large bowl; stir in onion mixture, tomatoes, and next 3 ingredients. Add toasted cornbread cubes, and toss to coat. Serve immediately.

skillet cornbread

makes: 8 servings hands-on time: 10 min. total time: 40 min.

2 tsp. canola oil
1¾ cups self-rising white cornmeal
    mix
2 cups nonfat buttermilk
¼ cup all-purpose flour
1 large egg, lightly beaten
2 Tbsp. butter, melted
1 Tbsp. sugar

1. Preheat oven to 425°. Coat bottom and sides of a 10-inch cast-iron skillet with canola oil; heat in oven 5 minutes. Meanwhile, whisk together cornmeal mix, buttermilk, flour, egg, melted butter, and sugar. Pour batter into hot skillet. Bake at 425° for 25 to 30 minutes, or until golden.

mango-spinach salad with warm bacon vinaigrette

This is a delicious partner for grilled fish. Don't forget fresh crusty bread to soak up every bit of the warm vinaigrette.

makes: 4 servings   hands-on time: 18 min.   total time: 18 min.

4   thick bacon slices, diced
½   medium-size red onion, thinly sliced
¼   cup red wine vinegar
1   Tbsp. lime juice
1   Tbsp. honey
1   (9-oz.) package fresh spinach
1   mango, peeled and diced
⅓   cup crumbled queso fresco (fresh Mexican cheese)
Salt and freshly ground pepper to taste

1. Cook bacon in a skillet over medium-high heat 6 to 8 minutes or until crisp; remove bacon, and drain on paper towels, reserving 1 Tbsp. drippings in skillet.

2. Sauté onion in hot drippings 2 to 3 minutes or until soft. Add vinegar, lime juice, and honey; cook 2 minutes, stirring to loosen particles from bottom of skillet.

3. Place spinach in a serving bowl. Add warm vinaigrette, and toss to coat. Top with mango, queso fresco, and bacon; season with salt and pepper to taste. Serve immediately.

TASTE OF SUMMER

HONEY

Moist, spreadable, and abundant, honey adds more than sweetness to your cooking—it adds a rich, unique flavor to foods. Because it's produced in so many places and in such different strengths and flavors, it's important to choose the best blend. The general rule states the lighter the color, the milder the flavor.

Y'ALL ENJOY

Derby Day

4 servings

Grilled Peach Salad

Kentucky Hot Browns *(page 149)*

Bakery cookies

Mint Julep bar *(page 282)*

grilled peach salad (pictured on opposite page, top left)

Gorgonzola cheese gets gooey and delicious melted over the grilled peaches in this amazing salad recipe. There's a perfect balance of salty and sweet goodness.

makes: 4 servings   hands-on time: 20 min   total time: 30 min.

1   cup pecans
4   large fresh, ripe peaches, halved
3   Tbsp. extra virgin olive oil, divided
Salt and freshly ground pepper to taste
1   (4-oz.) wedge Gorgonzola cheese, broken into 8 pieces
2   cups arugula
¼   cup honey*
2   Tbsp. finely chopped chives

1. Preheat oven to 350°. Bake pecans at 350° in a single layer in a shallow pan 10 to 12 minutes or until toasted and fragrant, stirring halfway through.

2. Preheat grill to 350° to 400° (medium-high) heat. Gently toss peach halves in 1 Tbsp. olive oil; sprinkle with salt and pepper to taste. Grill peaches, cut sides down, covered with grill lid, 2 to 3 minutes or until golden. Turn peaches, and place 1 cheese piece in center of each peach; grill, covered with grill lid, 2 to 3 minutes or until cheese begins to melt.

3. Toss arugula with remaining 2 Tbsp. olive oil and salt and pepper to taste. Arrange arugula on a serving platter; sprinkle with toasted pecans, and top with grilled peach halves. Drizzle peaches with honey, and sprinkle with chives.

*Aged balsamic vinegar may be substituted.

grilled shrimp salad with sweet tea vinaigrette

makes: 6 servings   hands-on time: 16 min.
total time: 1 hr., 6 min., including vinaigrette

1 cup coarsely chopped pecans	1 (6-oz.) bag mixed baby salad greens
1 lb. peeled, jumbo raw shrimp	Sweet Tea Vinaigrette
1 Tbsp. olive oil	Salt and freshly ground pepper to taste
2 large fresh peaches, cut into 8 wedges each	1 cup crumbled blue cheese

1. Preheat oven to 350°. Bake pecans at 350° in a single layer in a shallow pan 5 to 7 minutes or until lightly toasted and fragrant, stirring halfway through.

2. Preheat grill to 350° to 400° (medium-high) heat. Devein shrimp, if desired, and toss with olive oil. Grill shrimp, covered with grill lid, 2 to 3 minutes on each side or to desired degree of doneness. Grill peach wedges 1 to 2 minutes on each side or until grill marks appear.

3. Toss salad greens with Sweet Tea Vinaigrette; season with salt and pepper to taste, and top with grilled shrimp, peaches, blue cheese, and pecans. Serve immediately.

sweet tea vinaigrette

makes: about ¾ cup
hands-on time: 10 min.   total time: 45 min.

1 cup sweetened tea	¼ tsp. Dijon mustard
2 Tbsp. cider vinegar	Pinch of salt
¼ tsp. honey	6 Tbsp. canola oil

1. Bring tea to a boil in a saucepan over medium-low heat; reduce heat to low, and simmer 9 to 10 minutes or until reduced to ⅓ cup. Remove from heat; cool 20 minutes. Whisk in vinegar and next 3 ingredients. Whisk in oil slowly until blended.

Gulf Coast Catches

Nothing beats the sight of a shrimp boat gliding over Gulf Coast waters in the early morning light. On Mississippi Sound, where a small strand of islands keeps waves from rolling in, the water is calm and flat, reaching out to the horizon like a giant mirror sparkling in the sun. And the shrimp boats set across it each morning, heading out to the Gulf to cast their nets and try their luck. On State Highway 1 in coastal Louisiana—"L.A.1," the locals call it—you can follow a ribbon of canal that winds its way through tiny fishing towns where every other house has a shrimp boat docked out front, as if it were just another family vehicle. This road will take you to a place where the land fades into the water until you can't tell one from the other. And then there are the marinas—not the slick and polished kind aimed at tourists and leisure cruisers, but the hardworking variety. They're a maze of wooden piers, worn and weathered and maybe a little warped, but still there for the crossing. It's wonderful to walk out on a pier like that and just listen—to water slapping against barnacled posts; to the creak-creak of moorings straining against a shrimp boat as it rocks back and forth at the dock; to seagulls calling and wings flapping. As the birds explore the sky above, the fishermen pay their respects to the Gulf below. Another coastal adventure has begun.

VFL

STIR A SPELL

Y'ALL ENJOY

Summer Luncheon

6 servings

Mediterranean Chicken Salad

Watermelon-Peach Salsa and Tomatoes (*page 143*)

Assorted crackers

Mediterranean chicken salad

(pictured on opposite page, top left)

makes: 6 servings   hands-on time: 15 min.   total time: 35 min.

2   cups boiling water
1   cup uncooked bulgur wheat
1½ tsp. salt, divided
3   cups chopped cooked chicken
1   cup grape tomatoes, halved
2   garlic cloves, pressed
¾   cup chopped fresh parsley
½   cup bottled Caesar dressing
¼   cup finely chopped red onion
1   (4-oz.) package crumbled feta
1   medium cucumber, peeled and chopped
1   head Bibb lettuce

1. Combine boiling water, bulgur wheat, and 1 tsp. salt. Cover and let stand 20 minutes or until tender. Drain and rinse with cold water.

2. Combine bulgur wheat, chicken, next 7 ingredients, and remaining ½ tsp. salt. Serve over Bibb lettuce leaves.

Try This Twist!

◇ **Mediterranean chicken salad with rice:** Reduce salt to
◇ ½ tsp. Omit boiling water. Substitute 1 (6-oz.) package long-grain
◇ and wild rice mix for bulgur wheat. Prepare rice according to pack-
◇ age directions. Proceed with recipe as directed in Step 2.

refreshed

watermelon-peach salsa and tomatoes

(pictured on page 141, bottom right)

makes: 6 servings   hands-on time: 20 min.   total time: 20 min.

½   cup hot pepper jelly
1   Tbsp. lime zest
¼   cup fresh lime juice
2   cups seeded and diced fresh watermelon
1   cup peeled and diced fresh peaches
⅓   cup chopped fresh basil
⅓   cup chopped fresh chives
3   cups baby heirloom tomatoes
Salt and freshly ground pepper to taste

1. Whisk together pepper jelly, lime zest, and lime juice in a bowl; stir in watermelon and next 3 ingredients.

2. Cut heirloom tomatoes in half. Season halved baby tomatoes with salt and freshly ground pepper to taste; spoon into cocktail glasses. Top with salsa.

tortellini-and-tomato salad (pictured on opposite page)

makes: 6 servings   hands-on time: 20 min.   total time: 20 min.

2   (9-oz.) packages refrigerated cheese-filled tortellini
½   cup olive oil
½   cup freshly grated Parmesan cheese
3   Tbsp. fresh lemon juice
2   garlic cloves
1   tsp. Worcestershire sauce
½   tsp. salt
2   cups baby heirloom tomatoes, halved
1   cup fresh corn kernels
½   cup thinly sliced green onions
½   cup coarsely chopped fresh basil
Salt and freshly ground pepper to taste

1. Prepare tortellini according to package directions.

2. Meanwhile, process olive oil and next 5 ingredients in a blender until smooth. Toss olive oil mixture with hot cooked tortellini, tomatoes, and next 3 ingredients. Season with salt and pepper to taste.

crisp salads, cool sandwiches

GRAPES

It's hard to imagine a fruit more versatile than these flavorful berries. Grapes work well in salads, as well as in sorbets and pies. They're also nice in chicken dishes and salsas, and, of course, they're delicious in jams. But, sometimes they taste best of all eaten in handfuls by themselves. When it comes to selection, go for grapes with character. The most flavorful ones have seeds. Muscat grapes deliver sweet, musky flavor. Thompson seedless, found in many grocery stores, are best when allowed to ripen until they're yellow-green. You can use red and green seedless grapes interchangeably in recipes. Look for grapes that are plump, richly colored, and fully attached to their stems. Grapes will keep unwashed in a plastic bag in the refrigerator for up to 1 week.

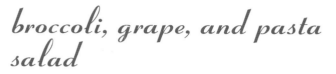

broccoli, grape, and pasta salad

If you're a broccoli salad fan, you'll love the combination of these colorful ingredients. Cook the pasta al dente so it's firm enough to hold its own when tossed with the tangy-sweet salad dressing.

makes: 6 to 8 servings
hands-on time: 25 min.   total time: 3 hr., 30 min.

1 cup chopped pecans	⅓ cup red wine vinegar
½ (16-oz.) package farfalle (bow-tie) pasta	1 tsp. salt
1 lb. fresh broccoli	2 cups seedless red grapes, halved
1 cup mayonnaise	8 cooked bacon slices, crumbled
⅓ cup sugar	
⅓ cup diced red onion	

1. Preheat oven to 350°. Bake pecans at 350° in a single layer in a shallow pan 5 to 7 minutes or until lightly toasted and fragrant, stirring halfway through.

2. Prepare pasta according to package directions.

3. Meanwhile, cut broccoli florets from stems, and separate florets into small pieces using tip of a paring knife. Peel away tough outer layer of stems, and finely chop stems.

4. Whisk together mayonnaise and next 4 ingredients in a large bowl; add broccoli, hot cooked pasta, and grapes, and stir to coat. Cover and chill 3 hours. Stir bacon and pecans into salad just before serving.

crisp salads, cool sandwiches

145

Kentucky Benedictine tea sandwiches

(pictured on opposite page, front left)

makes: 8 dozen   hands-on time: 15 min.   total time: 15 min.

2 (8-oz.) packages cream cheese, softened
1 cup peeled, seeded, and finely chopped cucumber
½ cup minced green onions
¼ cup chopped fresh dill
2 Tbsp. mayonnaise
½ tsp. salt
½ tsp. freshly ground pepper
48 white bread slices

1. Stir together first 7 ingredients. Spread mixture on 1 side of 24 bread slices; top with remaining 24 bread slices. Trim crusts from sandwiches; cut each sandwich into 4 triangles with a serrated knife.

mini muffulettas (pictured on opposite page, front right)

makes: 12 appetizer servings
hands-on time: 25 min.   total time: 25 min.

2 (16-oz.) jars mixed pickled vegetables
¾ cup pimiento-stuffed Spanish olives, chopped
2 Tbsp. bottled olive oil-and-vinegar dressing
12 small dinner rolls, cut in half
6 Swiss cheese slices, cut in half
12 thin deli ham slices
12 Genoa salami slices
6 provolone cheese slices, cut in half

1. Pulse pickled vegetables in a food processor 8 to 10 times or until finely chopped. Stir in olives and dressing.

2. Spread 1 heaping tablespoonful pickled vegetable mixture over cut side of each roll bottom. Top each with 1 Swiss cheese slice half, 1 ham slice, 1 salami slice, 1 provolone cheese slice half, and roll tops. Cover with plastic wrap. Serve immediately, or chill until ready to serve.

note: We tested with Mezzetta Italian Mix Giardiniera pickled vegetables and Newman's Own Olive Oil & Vinegar dressing.

Kentucky hot browns

Originally created in the 1920s at the Brown Hotel in Louisville, Kentucky, this Southern classic boasts turkey, bacon, cheese, and tomato on an open-faced sandwich covered with a rich Mornay sauce.

makes: 4 servings
hands-on time: 20 min.   total time: 35 min., including sauce

4   thick white bread slices
¾   lb. sliced roasted turkey
Mornay Sauce
1   cup (4 oz.) shredded Parmesan cheese
3   plum tomatoes, sliced
8   bacon slices, cooked

1. Preheat broiler with oven rack 6 inches from heat. Place bread slices on a baking sheet, and broil 1 to 2 minutes on each side or until toasted.

2. Arrange bread slices in 4 lightly greased broiler-safe individual baking dishes. Top bread with turkey slices. Pour hot Mornay Sauce over turkey. Sprinkle with Parmesan cheese.

3. Broil 3 to 4 minutes or until bubbly and lightly browned; remove from oven. Top sandwiches with tomatoes and bacon. Serve immediately.

mornay sauce

makes: 4 cups   hands-on time: 10 min.   total time: 10 min.

½   cup butter
⅓   cup all-purpose flour
3½ cups milk
½   cup (2 oz.) shredded Parmesan cheese
¼   tsp. salt
¼   tsp. pepper

1. Melt butter in a 3-qt. saucepan over medium-high heat. Whisk in flour; cook, whisking constantly, 1 minute. Gradually whisk in milk. Bring to a boil, and cook, whisking constantly, 1 to 2 minutes or until thickened. Whisk in Parmesan cheese, salt, and pepper.

crisp salads, cool sandwiches

149

flank steak sandwiches with Brie

makes: 6 servings   hands-on time: 42 min.   total time: 52 min.

2   large sweet onions
4   Tbsp. olive oil, divided
½   tsp. salt, divided
½   tsp. freshly ground pepper,
     divided
3   red bell peppers
6   (2- to 3-oz.) ciabatta or deli
     rolls, split
5   oz. Brie, rind removed
Herb-Marinated Flank Steak
1½ cups loosely packed arugula
6   Tbsp. mayonnaise

1. Preheat grill to 400° to 500° (high) heat. Cut onion into ¼-inch-thick slices. Brush with 1 Tbsp. olive oil, and sprinkle with ¼ tsp. salt and ¼ tsp. pepper. Cut bell peppers into 1-inch-wide strips. Place pepper strips in a large bowl, and drizzle with 1 Tbsp. olive oil. Sprinkle with remaining ¼ tsp. salt and ¼ tsp. pepper; toss to coat.

2. Grill onion and bell pepper strips, covered with grill lid, 7 to 10 minutes on each side or until lightly charred and tender.

3. Brush cut sides of rolls with remaining 2 Tbsp. olive oil, and grill, cut sides down, without grill lid, 1 to 2 minutes or until lightly browned and toasted.

4. Spread Brie on cut sides of roll bottoms; top with onion, bell pepper strips, steak, and arugula. Spread mayonnaise on cut sides of roll tops. Place roll tops, mayonnaise sides down, on top of onion, pressing lightly.

herb-marinated flank steak

makes: 6 servings
hands-on time: 33 min.   total time: 1 hr., 12 min.

½   small sweet onion, minced
3   garlic cloves, minced
¼   cup olive oil
2   Tbsp. chopped fresh basil
1   Tbsp. chopped fresh thyme
1   Tbsp. chopped fresh rosemary
1   tsp. salt
½   tsp. dried crushed red pepper
1¾ lb. flank steak
1   lemon, halved

1. Place first 8 ingredients in a 2-gal. zip-top plastic freezer bag, and squeeze bag to combine. Add steak; seal bag, and chill 30 minutes to 1 hour and 30 minutes. Remove steak from marinade, discarding marinade.

2. Preheat grill to 400° to 500° (high) heat. Grill steak, covered with grill lid, 9 minutes on each side or to desired degree of doneness. Remove from grill; squeeze juice from lemon over steak. Let stand 10 minutes. Cut diagonally across the grain into thin slices.

refreshed

best turkey burgers

makes: 6 servings
hands-on time: 32 min.   total time: 3 hr., including buns

2   lb. lean ground turkey breast
1   tsp. salt
1   tsp. lemon zest
½   cup mayonnaise
¼   cup chopped fresh parsley
Homemade Hamburger Buns

1. Preheat grill to 350° to 400° (medium-high) heat. Combine first 5 ingredients gently. Shape mixture into 6 (5-inch) patties.

2. Grill, covered with grill lid, 6 to 7 minutes on each side or until a meat thermometer inserted into thickest portion registers 160°. Serve on Homemade Hamburger Buns.

Try This Twist!

green tomato-feta burgers: Stir 1 (4-oz.) container crumbled feta cheese, 1 Tbsp. finely minced red onion, and 1 tsp. minced oregano into meat mixture. Proceed as directed. Top each burger with sliced pickled green tomatoes, lettuce, thinly sliced cucumber, a pinch of dried crushed red pepper, and a fresh dill sprig.

homemade hamburger buns

makes: 12 buns
hands-on time: 15 min.   total time: 2 hr., 35 min.

1   (48-oz.) package frozen white bread dough loaves
1   large egg
2   Tbsp. sesame seeds or poppy seeds (optional)

1. Let dough stand at room temperature for 15 minutes. Cut dough into 12 equal portions. Place dough portions on a lightly greased 15- x 10-inch jelly-roll pan. Let rise in a warm place (85°), free from drafts, 30 minutes or until doubled in bulk.

2. Shape each dough portion into a 5-inch circle, and place on a lightly greased jelly-roll pan. Whisk together egg and 2 Tbsp. water. Brush dough lightly with egg mixture; sprinkle with sesame seeds, if desired.

3. Let rise in a warm place (85°), free from drafts, 1 hour or until doubled in bulk.

4. Preheat oven to 400°. Bake rolls at 400° for 20 to 22 minutes or until browned. Let stand 15 minutes. Cut rolls in half crosswise; toast, if desired.

best beef burgers

Let ground beef stand at room temperature for 10 minutes before grilling.

makes: 6 servings
hands-on time: 28 min.   total time: 3 hr., including buns

1   lb. ground sirloin
1   lb. ground chuck
1   tsp. salt
½   tsp. freshly ground pepper
Homemade Hamburger Buns

1. Preheat grill to 350° to 400° (medium-high) heat. Combine first 4 ingredients gently. Shape mixture into 6 (5-inch) patties.

2. Grill, covered with grill lid, 4 to 5 minutes on each side or to desired degree of doneness. Serve on Homemade Hamburger Buns.

Try These Twists!

pimiento cheese-bacon burgers: Stir ¼ cup mixed chopped fresh herbs (such as basil, mint, and oregano) into meat mixture. Proceed as directed. Top each burger with pimiento cheese, cooked bacon slices, lettuce, and tomato slices.

sun-dried tomato-pesto burgers: Stir 1 (3-oz.) package sun-dried tomato halves, chopped, and 1 garlic clove, pressed, into meat mixture. Proceed as directed. Top each burger with refrigerated pesto, sliced goat cheese, and sliced pepperoncini salad peppers.

crisp salads, cool sandwiches

blt Benedict with avocado-tomato relish

Sunny-side up or sliced boiled eggs would work just as well as poached eggs for this dish you've got to try.

makes: 6 servings
hands-on time: 23 min.   **total time: 23 min.**

1   cup halved grape tomatoes
1   avocado, diced
1   Tbsp. chopped fresh basil
1   garlic clove, minced
2   Tbsp. extra virgin olive oil
Salt and freshly ground pepper to taste
1   Tbsp. red wine vinegar, divided
6   large eggs
¼   cup mayonnaise
6   (¾-inch-thick) bakery bread slices, toasted
3   cups firmly packed arugula
12 thick bacon slices, cooked

1. Combine tomatoes and next 5 ingredients and 2½ tsp. red wine vinegar in a small bowl.

2. Add water to depth of 3 inches in a large saucepan. Bring to a boil; reduce heat, and maintain at a light simmer. Add remaining ½ tsp. red wine vinegar. Break eggs, and slip into water, 1 at a time, as close as possible to surface. Simmer 3 to 5 minutes or to desired degree of doneness. Remove with a slotted spoon. Trim edges, if desired.

3. Spread mayonnaise on 1 side of each bread slice. Layer each with ½ cup arugula, 2 bacon slices, and 1 egg. Top with tomato mixture.

country ham, turkey, and chard club

Maple-glazed turkey and sweet gherkin pickles offset the salty country ham in this piled-high sandwich. Tear the leaves of Swiss chard as needed to fit on the sandwiches.

makes: 4 servings hands-on time: 12 min. total time: 16 min.

½ (10-oz.) package sliced country ham (about 4 slices)
1 cup mayonnaise
2 Tbsp. coarse-grained Dijon mustard
12 hearty white bread slices, toasted
8 (1-oz.) deli maple-glazed turkey breast slices
8 (1-oz.) Cheddar cheese slices
8 tomato slices
4 large Swiss chard leaves
8 cooked bacon slices

1. Cook ham according to package directions.

2. Stir together mayonnaise and mustard in a small bowl. Spread 1 side of bread slices with mayonnaise mixture. Layer 4 bread slices, mayonnaise mixture sides up, with 1 slice turkey, 1 slice ham, 1 slice cheese, and 1 slice tomato. Top with 4 bread slices, mayonnaise mixture sides up; layer with 1 leaf Swiss chard, 1 slice tomato, 2 slices bacon, 1 slice turkey, and 1 slice cheese. Top with remaining 4 bread slices, mayonnaise mixture sides down. Cut sandwiches in quarters, and secure with wooden picks.

TASTE OF SPRING

SWISS CHARD

Add a little unique flavor to your sandwiches by substituting Swiss chard for the lettuce. This vegetable has the flavor of an intense spinach and is often used in Mediterranean cooking. When selecting, look for leaves that are fresh without any brown spots and stalks that are tender. Store it in the refrigerator for about 2 to 3 days and wait to wash it until you are ready to use.

hushed crab cake sandwich

Two seafood favorites, crab cakes and hush puppies, unite in one fabulous sandwich.

makes: 6 servings
hands-on time: 14 min.   total time: 1 hr., 50 min.

1 lb. fresh lump crabmeat, drained
½ cup chopped green onions
3 Tbsp. mayonnaise
1 Tbsp. Dijon mustard
1 Tbsp. fresh lemon juice
1 tsp. Worcestershire sauce
12 round buttery crackers, crushed (about ½ cup)
1 egg yolk
1¼ tsp. Old Bay seasoning, divided
Parchment paper
1 cup self-rising yellow cornmeal mix
½ cup self-rising flour
¾ cup beer
1 large egg, lightly beaten
Canola oil
3 Tbsp. butter, softened
6 French hamburger buns, split
Toppings: green leaf lettuce leaves, bottled rémoulade, tomato slices, sliced green onions

1. Pick crabmeat, removing any bits of shell. Stir together crabmeat, next 7 ingredients, and ¼ tsp. Old Bay seasoning in a large bowl. Shape mixture into 6 (3-inch) patties; place on a parchment paper-lined baking sheet. Cover with plastic wrap; freeze 1 hour or until firm.

2. Stir together cornmeal mix, flour, and remaining 1 tsp. Old Bay seasoning in a large bowl. Stir together beer and egg; add to dry mixture, stirring just until moistened. Let stand 5 minutes.

3. Pour oil to depth of 2 inches into a Dutch oven; heat to 350°. Dip crab cakes into batter, shaking off excess. Fry crab cakes, in 2 batches, 4 minutes on each side or until golden brown. Drain on a wire rack over paper towels.

4. Meanwhile, preheat broiler with oven rack 5½ inches from heat. Spread butter on cut sides of buns; place buns on a baking sheet. Broil 1 minute or until toasted. Serve crab cakes on buns with desired toppings.

note: We tested with Publix Deli French Hamburger Buns.

fried catfish po'boys

Because smaller, sandwich-size fillets are difficult to find in markets, we opted for big, meaty fillets and cut them in half before breading and frying.

makes: 4 servings   hands-on time: 38 min.   total time: 38 min.

3   Tbsp. mayonnaise
2   Tbsp. white wine vinegar
1   Tbsp. sour cream
1   Tbsp. Cajun seasoning, divided
1½ tsp. salt, divided
½   tsp. pepper, divided
1   (10-oz.) package finely
     shredded cabbage
½   cup milk
1   large egg
¾   cup all-purpose flour
¾   cup plain yellow cornmeal
2   (8-oz.) catfish fillets, cut in half
     crosswise
Canola oil
1   (12-oz.) French bread loaf
Toppings: tomato slices, onion
     slices, and dill pickle chips

1. Stir together first 3 ingredients, 2 tsp. Cajun seasoning, ½ tsp. salt, and ¼ tsp. pepper in a medium bowl. Add cabbage, stirring until well coated. Cover and chill.

2. Whisk together milk and egg in a shallow dish or pie plate. Stir together flour, cornmeal, remaining 1 tsp. Cajun seasoning, remaining 1 tsp. salt, and remaining ¼ tsp. pepper in another shallow dish or pie plate. Dip catfish in egg mixture; dredge in cornmeal mixture.

3. Pour oil to depth of 1 inch into a large heavy skillet; heat to 350°. Fry catfish, in batches, 2 to 3 minutes on each side or until golden brown and done. Drain on a wire rack over paper towels.

4. Preheat broiler with oven rack 5½ inches from heat. Cut bread loaf crosswise into 4 equal portions; cut each portion in half horizontally. Place bread, cut sides up, on a baking sheet. Broil 1 to 2 minutes or until toasted.

5. Place catfish fillets on bottom halves of bread; top with slaw mixture, tomato slices, onion slices, and pickles. Cover with top halves of bread.

WARMTH

Texas-style barbecued beef brisket

makes: 4 to 6 servings
hands-on time: 20 min.   total time: 7 hr., 40 min.

1	large sweet onion, sliced
3	garlic cloves, chopped
1	Tbsp. chili powder
1	Tbsp. jarred beef soup base
1	Tbsp. Worcestershire sauce
1	tsp. ground cumin
½	tsp. pepper
1½	tsp. hickory liquid smoke
1	(2- to 3-lb.) beef brisket flat, trimmed
¼	cup beer
3	Tbsp. bottled chili sauce

1. Lightly grease a 6-qt. slow cooker; add onion and garlic. Stir together chili powder and next 5 ingredients. Rub over brisket; place brisket over onion mixture in slow cooker.

2. Whisk together beer and chili sauce. Slowly pour mixture around brisket (to avoid removing spices from brisket).

3. Cover and cook on LOW 7 to 8 hours (or on HIGH 4 to 5 hours) or until fork-tender. Uncover and let stand in slow cooker 20 minutes.

4. Remove brisket from slow cooker; cut brisket across the grain into thin slices. Return brisket to slow cooker; spoon pan juices over meat.

SIT A SPELL

The Jumbo State

Nobody has more state pride than Texans. They're proud of their big sky and vast landscape. They're proud of their cattle ranches, of Big Tex and Big D, and Texas-style barbecue—which tends toward beef in a big way. They're even proud of their dramatic weather, particularly their tolerance for heat, which gets extreme during the prime brisket months of summer. And the thing is, Texas pride is contagious. I'm an Alabama girl, but I lived in Texas for three years. I remember when my mother called during the summer to ask me what kind of weather we were having. "We're having a little cold snap," I said, with a swagger in my voice. "It dipped way down into the nineties." Mama grew up on a cotton farm, and she wondered if I had seen any fields in Texas. "Cotton fields?" I said. "You wanna hear about some Texas cotton fields? Why they're so big, these farmers head down a row on Tuesday, and they don't even have to turn around till Thursday." Mama said she knew something else that was getting pretty big—my head. She said it might be time for me to come on home . . . before I got entirely too big for my britches.

VFL

grits and grillades

makes: 6 servings
hands-on time: 30 min.   total time: 3 hr., 30 min.

1½ lb. top round steak (½ inch thick), trimmed
3   Tbsp. all-purpose flour
2   tsp. Creole seasoning
2   Tbsp. vegetable oil
1   (14½-oz.) can fire-roasted diced tomatoes
1   (10-oz.) package frozen diced onion, red and green bell pepper, and celery, thawed
3   garlic cloves, pressed
Asiago Cheese Grits

1. Place steak between 2 sheets of heavy-duty plastic wrap, and flatten to ¼-inch thickness using a rolling pin or flat side of a meat mallet; cut into 2-inch squares.

2. Combine flour and Creole seasoning in a large zip-top plastic freezer bag. Add steak; seal bag, and shake to coat.

3. Heat 1 Tbsp. oil in a large skillet over medium-high heat. Add half of steak, and cook 2 to 3 minutes on each side or until browned; transfer steak to a 4- or 5-qt. lightly greased slow cooker. Repeat procedure with remaining oil and steak. Add tomatoes and next 2 ingredients to slow cooker, and stir.

4. Cover and cook on HIGH 3 hours or until steak is tender. Meanwhile, prepare Asiago Cheese Grits. Serve steak mixture over grits.

asiago cheese grits

If you've never experienced the fresh corn taste of stone-ground grits, the first intoxicating forkful will make you a believer.

makes: 6 servings
hands-on time: 5 min.   total time: 2 hr., 35 min.

1   cup uncooked stone-ground grits
½   cup (2 oz.) shredded Asiago cheese
1   Tbsp. butter
½   tsp. salt
½   tsp. freshly ground pepper

1. Stir together grits and 3 cups water in a 3-qt. slow cooker. Let stand 1 to 2 minutes, allowing grits to settle to bottom; tilt slow cooker slightly, and skim off solids using a fine wire-mesh strainer. Cover and cook on HIGH 2½ to 3 hours or until grits are creamy and tender, stirring every 45 minutes.

2. Stir in cheese and remaining ingredients.

GREEN BEANS

A bushel of green beans conjures up thoughts in the South
of sitting on back porches in the
summertime stringing pole beans.
There are many varieties of this
versatile legume ranging from
svelte haricots verts to large wax
beans. When selecting them, look
for dark-colored, slender green
beans. Avoid green beans that are
spotty. Green beans should last for
about 10 days in the refrigerator
when wrapped tightly in plastic
wrap. Summer is their prime
time, but they're available year-
round. In fact, in many families it
just wouldn't be Thanksgiving or
Christmas without a green
bean casserole.

grilled fillets with pecans and green bean ravioli

makes: 4 servings   hands-on time: 22 min.   total time: 36 min.

4   (4-oz.) beef tenderloin fillets
1   tsp. salt
½   tsp. freshly ground pepper
1   (20-oz.) package refrigerated cheese-filled ravioli
1   (8-oz.) package fresh small green beans
½   cup chopped pecans
½   cup butter
3   garlic cloves, thinly sliced
1   Tbsp. chopped fresh sage
½   cup (2 oz.) shaved Parmesan cheese

1. Preheat grill to 350° to 400° (medium-high) heat. Sprinkle fillets with salt and pepper. Grill, covered with grill lid, 5 to 8 minutes on each side or until a meat thermometer inserted into thickest portion registers 145°. Let stand 10 minutes.

2. Cook ravioli and green beans in boiling water to cover in a Dutch oven 4 to 5 minutes or until green beans are crisp-tender. Drain.

3. Heat pecans in a large nonstick skillet over medium-low heat, stirring often, 2 to 3 minutes or until toasted and fragrant. Remove from skillet; wipe skillet clean. Melt butter in skillet over medium heat. Add garlic, and sauté 5 to 7 minutes or until garlic is caramel colored and butter begins to brown. Remove from heat, and stir in sage, hot pasta mixture, and pecans. Sprinkle with cheese. Serve immediately with fillets.

tomato 'n' beef casserole with polenta crust

makes: 6 servings   hands-on time: 20 min.   total time: 55 min.

1   tsp. salt
1   cup plain yellow cornmeal
½   tsp. Montreal steak seasoning
1   cup (4 oz.) shredded sharp
    Cheddar cheese, divided
1   lb. ground chuck
1   cup chopped onion
1   medium zucchini, cut in half
    lengthwise and sliced (about
    2 cups)
1   Tbsp. olive oil
2   (14½-oz.) cans petite diced
    tomatoes, drained
1   (6-oz.) can tomato paste
2   Tbsp. chopped fresh flat-leaf
    parsley

1. Preheat oven to 350°. Bring 3 cups water and 1 tsp. salt to a boil in a 2-qt. saucepan over medium-high heat. Whisk in cornmeal; reduce heat to low, and simmer, whisking constantly, 3 minutes or until thickened. Remove from heat, and stir in steak seasoning and ¼ cup Cheddar cheese. Spread cornmeal mixture into a lightly greased 11- x 7-inch baking dish.

2. Brown ground chuck in a large nonstick skillet over medium-high heat, stirring often, 10 minutes or until meat crumbles and is no longer pink; drain and transfer to a bowl.

3. Sauté onion and zucchini in hot oil in skillet over medium heat 5 minutes or until crisp-tender. Stir in beef, tomatoes, and tomato paste; simmer, stirring often, 10 minutes. Pour beef mixture over cornmeal crust. Sprinkle with remaining ¾ cup cheese.

4. Bake at 350° for 30 minutes or until bubbly. Sprinkle casserole with parsley just before serving.

Try This Twist!

◊ **Italian sausage casserole with polenta crust:** Substitute Italian sausage for ground chuck and Italian six-cheese blend for Cheddar cheese. Prepare recipe as directed, sautéing 1 medium-size green bell pepper, chopped, with onion in Step 3.

sage-and-pecan pork tenderloin cutlets

makes: 4 servings   hands-on time: 35 min.   total time: 51 min.

1   cup red wine vinegar
5   Tbsp. seedless blackberry
     preserves
½   tsp. salt
1   lb. pork tenderloin
¾   cup fine, dry breadcrumbs
½   cup finely chopped pecans
2   tsp. rubbed sage
2   large eggs, beaten
4   tsp. olive oil
Garnishes: fresh blackberries,
     fresh sage leaves

1. Bring vinegar to a boil in a small saucepan over medium-high heat. Reduce heat to medium, and cook 6 minutes or until reduced by half. Stir in preserves, and cook 5 minutes. Stir in salt.

2. Remove silver skin from tenderloin, leaving a thin layer of fat. Cut pork into 8 slices. Place pork between 2 sheets of plastic wrap, and flatten to ¼-inch thickness, using a rolling pin or flat side of a meat mallet.

3. Stir together breadcrumbs, pecans, and sage in a shallow bowl.

4. Dredge pork in breadcrumb mixture, dip in beaten eggs, and dredge again in breadcrumb mixture.

5. Cook 4 pork slices in 2 tsp. hot oil in a large nonstick skillet over medium heat 8 minutes or until done, turning every 2 minutes. Repeat procedure with remaining pork and oil. Serve with vinegar mixture, and garnish, if desired.

TASTE OF SUMMER

BLACKBERRIES

Plump, freshly picked berries warmed by the summer sun melt in your mouth, tickle your taste buds, and temporarily turn your tongue purple. When selecting blackberries, look for plump, well-colored berries with hulls detached. If hulls are still intact, the berries were picked too early. Fresh blackberries are best stored in the refrigerator for up to a week.

roasted pork belly with peaches and arugula

The strong, peppery flavor of arugula mixes well with the sweetness of the peaches and saltiness of the pork belly in this salad.

makes: 8 servings
hands-on time: 30 min.   total time: 4 hr., 15 min.

1	(3½- to 4-lb.) pork belly
1	Tbsp. kosher salt
2	tsp. freshly ground pepper
1	large sweet onion, chopped
2	celery ribs, chopped
5	garlic cloves, crushed
6	fresh thyme sprigs
1	Tbsp. extra virgin olive oil
4	to 6 peaches, peeled and cut into 6 wedges each
2	Tbsp. sherry vinegar
2	Tbsp. honey
1	tsp. chopped fresh thyme
4	cups loosely packed arugula

1. Preheat oven to 300°. Make ¼-inch-deep cuts in fattiest side of pork. Rub pork with kosher salt and freshly ground pepper. Arrange onion and next 3 ingredients in a large roasting pan; drizzle with oil, stirring to coat. Place pork, fattiest side up, on vegetables in pan.

2. Bake at 300° for 3½ to 4 hours or until tender. Let stand 10 minutes. Remove pork from pan, reserving 1 Tbsp. drippings. Discard remaining drippings and vegetables.

3. Cook pork in a 12-inch cast-iron skillet over medium heat 3 to 5 minutes on each side or until browned and crisp.

4. Stir together peaches and next 3 ingredients. Heat reserved 1 Tbsp. drippings in a large skillet over medium heat. Cook peach mixture in hot drippings, stirring often, 3 to 5 minutes or until thoroughly heated. Season with additional salt and pepper to taste. Slice pork, and serve with warm peaches and arugula.

grilled porterhouse pork chops with peach agrodolce

makes: 4 servings
hands-on time: 15 min.   total time: 1 hr., 25 min.

4   (1½-inch-thick) porterhouse pork chops (about 2½ lb.)
1   Tbsp. olive oil
¾   tsp. kosher salt
½   tsp. freshly ground pepper
Peach Agrodolce

1. Let pork stand at room temperature 30 minutes. Light 1 side of grill, and preheat to 350° to 400° (medium-high) heat; leave other side unlit. Brush pork with olive oil, and sprinkle with salt and pepper.

2. Grill pork over lit side of grill, covered with grill lid, 4 minutes on each side; transfer pork to unlit side, and grill, covered with grill lid, 10 minutes on each side or until a meat thermometer registers 145°. Let stand 5 minutes. Arrange pork on a serving platter, and serve with Peach Agrodolce.

peach agrodolce

makes: 1½ cups   hands-on time: 15 min.   total time: 15 min.

2   Tbsp. raisins
2   Tbsp. tawny port wine
1   Tbsp. chopped fresh parsley
1   Tbsp. balsamic vinegar
1   Tbsp. olive oil
2   large fresh, ripe peaches, peeled and diced into 1-inch pieces
Salt and freshly ground pepper to taste

1. Cook raisins, port, and 2 Tbsp. water in a small saucepan over medium heat, stirring occasionally, 5 minutes. Remove from heat; whisk in parsley, vinegar, and oil. Stir in peaches, and season with salt and pepper to taste.

main dishes

177

Y'ALL ENJOY

Sunday Dinner

8 servings

Bourbon-Brown Sugar Tenderloin

Home-style Green Bean Casserole *(page 52)*

Mashed potatoes

Sweet Green Tomato Corn Muffins *(page 51)*

bourbon-brown sugar tenderloin

(pictured on opposite page, top left)

makes: 6 to 8 servings
hands-on time: 30 min.   total time: 8 hr., 30 min.

2   (1-lb.) pork tenderloins*
¼   cup firmly packed dark brown sugar
¼   cup minced green onions
¼   cup bourbon
¼   cup soy sauce
¼   cup Dijon mustard
½   tsp. freshly ground pepper
½   tsp. cornstarch
Garnish: sliced green onions

1. Remove silver skin from tenderloins, leaving a thin layer of fat. Combine brown sugar and next 5 ingredients in a large zip-top plastic freezer bag; add pork. Seal bag, and chill 8 to 18 hours, turning bag occasionally. Remove pork from marinade, reserving marinade.

2. Preheat grill to 350° to 400° (medium-high) heat. Grill pork, covered with grill lid, 8 minutes on each side or until a meat thermometer inserted into thickest portion registers 145°. Remove from grill, and let stand 10 minutes.

3. Meanwhile, combine reserved marinade and cornstarch in a saucepan. Bring to a boil over medium heat; cook, stirring constantly, 1 minute. Cut pork diagonally into thin slices, and arrange on a serving platter; drizzle with warm sauce. Garnish, if desired.

*1½ lb. flank steak may be substituted. Reduce grill time to 6 to 8 minutes on each side or to desired degree of doneness.

pecan-crusted chicken and tortellini with herbed butter sauce

makes: 4 servings   hands-on time: 30 min.   total time: 30 min.

2   (9-oz.) packages refrigerated
      cheese-filled tortellini
4   (4-oz.) chicken breast cutlets
½   tsp. salt
¼   tsp. freshly ground pepper
¾   cup finely chopped pecans
1   large egg, lightly beaten
3   Tbsp. olive oil
½   cup butter
3   garlic cloves, thinly sliced
3   Tbsp. chopped fresh basil
3   Tbsp. chopped fresh parsley
¼   cup (1 oz.) shredded
      Parmesan cheese
Garnish: fresh basil leaves

1. Prepare tortellini according to package directions. Keep warm.

2. Meanwhile, sprinkle chicken with salt and pepper. Place pecans in a shallow bowl. Place egg in a second bowl. Dip chicken in egg, allowing excess to drip off. Dredge chicken in pecans, pressing firmly to adhere.

3. Cook chicken in hot oil in a large nonstick skillet over medium-high heat 2 minutes on each side or desired degree of doneness. Remove from skillet; wipe skillet clean.

4. Melt butter in skillet over medium heat. Add garlic, and sauté 5 to 7 minutes or until garlic is caramel colored and butter begins to turn golden brown. Immediately remove from heat, and stir in basil, parsley, and hot cooked tortellini. Sprinkle with cheese. Serve immediately with chicken. Garnish, if desired.

TASTE OF SUMMER

BASIL

Summer is basil's best season, but the fragrant herb is available year-round in supermarkets. Much like tomatoes, basil is far superior when it's grown and picked in season. Look for basil that isn't wilted and doesn't have dark spots. And if you're growing your own, be sure to harvest it on a sunny day, because the sun will bring out the essential oils that won't be present otherwise.

pepper and chicken nachos

Grilled peppers add a crunchy and flavorful base for a twist on this South-western favorite. If you have a little extra time, you can grill chicken breasts for this dish while you're grilling the peppers.

makes: 4 servings   hands-on time: 18 min.   total time: 37 min.

4   garlic cloves, pressed
¼   cup cider vinegar
⅓   cup olive oil
½   tsp. ground cumin
½   tsp. salt
½   tsp. freshly ground pepper
4   medium bell peppers, cut into 2-inch pieces
2   cups chopped deli-roasted chicken
1   (15½-oz.) can black-eyed peas, drained and rinsed
1   (7.5-oz.) package sliced sharp Cheddar cheese
⅓   cup loosely packed fresh cilantro leaves

1. Preheat grill to 350° to 400° (medium-high) heat. Combine garlic and next 5 ingredients. Reserve 3 Tbsp. garlic mixture. Pour remaining garlic mixture into a large shallow dish; add peppers, turning to coat. Cover and chill 15 minutes, turning once. Remove peppers from marinade, reserving marinade for basting.

2. Grill peppers, covered with grill lid, 8 to 10 minutes or until peppers blister and are tender, turning occasionally and basting with marinade.

3. Preheat broiler with oven rack 4 inches from heat. Combine chicken and peas with reserved 3 Tbsp. garlic mixture. Place peppers in a single layer on a lightly greased rack in an aluminum foil-lined broiler pan. Quarter cheese slices. Top each pepper with chicken mixture and 1 cheese quarter.

4. Broil 4 to 5 minutes or until cheese melts. Remove from oven, sprinkle with cilantro, and serve immediately.

grilled chicken with fresh corncakes

makes: 4 servings
hands-on time: 15 min.   total time: 56 min.

3   lemons
2   garlic cloves, pressed
⅓   cup olive oil
1   tsp. Dijon mustard
¼   tsp. pepper
1½ tsp. salt, divided
3   skinned and boned chicken
    breasts
3   ears fresh corn, husks
    removed
1   Tbsp. olive oil
1   (6-oz.) package buttermilk
    cornbread mix
¼   cup chopped fresh basil
8   cooked thick hickory-smoked
    bacon slices
2   cups loosely packed arugula

1. Preheat grill to 350° to 400° (medium-high) heat. Grate zest from lemons to equal 1 Tbsp. Cut lemons in half; squeeze juice from lemons into a measuring cup to equal ¼ cup.

2. Whisk together lemon zest, lemon juice, garlic, next 3 ingredients, and 1 tsp. salt. Reserve ¼ cup lemon mixture. Pour remaining lemon mixture in a large zip-top plastic freezer bag; add chicken. Seal and chill 15 minutes, turning once. Remove chicken from marinade, discarding marinade.

3. Brush corn with 1 Tbsp. olive oil; sprinkle with remaining ½ tsp. salt.

4. Grill chicken and corn, covered with grill lid, 20 minutes, turning chicken once, and turning corn every 4 to 5 minutes. Remove chicken, and cover. Hold each grilled cob upright on a cutting board, and carefully cut downward, cutting kernels from cob.

5. Stir together cornbread mix and ⅔ cup water in a small bowl until smooth. Stir in basil and 1 cup grilled corn kernels. Pour about ¼ cup batter for each corncake onto a hot, lightly greased griddle. Cook cakes 3 to 4 minutes or until tops are covered with bubbles and edges look dry and cooked; turn and cook other side.

6. Thinly slice chicken. To serve, place 2 corncakes on each plate, top with chicken and 2 bacon slices. Toss arugula with reserved lemon mixture. Place arugula mixture on bacon, and sprinkle with remaining corn kernels.

sweet tea-brined chicken

For the tastiest chicken ever, brine a whole cut-up chicken in the South's signature beverage—sweet tea with lemon.

makes: 6 to 8 servings
hands-on time: 30 min.
total time: 2 hr., 35 min., plus 1 day for marinating

2 family-size tea bags
½ cup firmly packed light brown sugar
¼ cup kosher salt
1 small sweet onion, thinly sliced
1 lemon, thinly sliced
3 garlic cloves, halved
2 (6-inch) fresh rosemary sprigs
1 Tbsp. freshly cracked pepper
2 cups ice cubes
1 (3 ½- to 4-lb.) cut-up whole chicken
Garnish: lemon wedges

1. Bring 4 cups water to a boil in a 3-qt. heavy saucepan; add tea bags. Remove from heat; cover and steep 10 minutes.

2. Discard tea bags. Stir in sugar and next 6 ingredients, stirring until sugar dissolves. Cool completely (about 45 minutes); stir in ice. (Mixture should be cold before adding chicken.)

3. Place tea mixture and chicken in a large zip-top plastic freezer bag; seal. Place bag in a shallow baking dish, and chill 24 hours. Remove chicken from marinade, discarding marinade; pat chicken dry with paper towels.

4. Light 1 side of grill, and preheat to 300° to 350° (medium) heat; leave other side unlit. Place chicken, skin side down, over unlit side, and grill, covered with grill lid, 20 minutes. Turn chicken, and grill, covered with grill lid, 40 to 50 minutes or to desired degree of doneness. Transfer chicken, skin side down, to lit side of grill, and grill 2 to 3 minutes or until skin is crispy. Let stand 5 minutes before serving. Garnish, if desired.

Y'ALL ENJOY

Southern Supper

6 servings

Hot Sauce Fried Chicken with Pickled Okra Slaw

Biscuits

Easy Skillet Apple Pie *(page 213)*

Sweet tea

---

hot sauce fried chicken with pickled okra slaw (pictured on opposite page, top left)

makes: 6 servings   hands-on time: 35 min.   total time: 35 min.

6   (4-oz.) chicken breast cutlets
1½ tsp. salt, divided
¾   tsp. pepper, divided
1¼ cups all-purpose flour
30 saltine crackers, crushed
½   tsp. baking powder
2   large eggs, lightly beaten
⅓   cup hot sauce
Peanut oil
½   cup sour cream
½   tsp. sugar
1   (16-oz.) package shredded coleslaw mix
½   cup sliced pickled okra
1   (4-oz.) jar diced pimiento, drained
Hot sauce

1. Sprinkle chicken with ½ tsp. salt and ½ tsp. pepper. Place ½ cup flour in a shallow dish. Stir together cracker crumbs, baking powder, and remaining ¾ cup flour in a second shallow dish. Whisk together eggs and hot sauce in a third shallow dish. Dredge chicken in flour, dip in egg mixture, and dredge in cracker mixture, pressing to adhere.

2. Pour oil to depth of 1 inch into a 10-inch cast-iron skillet; heat to 360°. Fry half of chicken 3 to 4 minutes. Turn and fry 2 to 3 minutes or until golden brown and desired degree of doneness. Repeat procedure with remaining half of chicken.

3. Stir together sour cream, sugar, and remaining 1 tsp. salt and ¼ tsp. pepper. Toss together coleslaw mix, pickled okra, diced pimiento, and sour cream mixture. Serve slaw and chicken with additional hot sauce.

warmth

188

skillet roasted okra and shrimp

makes: 6 servings   hands-on time: 30 min.   total time: 30 min.

1   lb. unpeeled, large raw shrimp
3   cups (about 8 oz.) fresh okra,
     cut in half lengthwise
3   Tbsp. olive oil, divided
1   pt. heirloom cherry tomatoes
3   large garlic cloves, thinly sliced
½   tsp. dried crushed red
     pepper
Salt and freshly ground pepper to
     taste

1. Peel shrimp; devein, if desired.

2. Sauté okra in 1 Tbsp. hot oil in a large cast-iron skillet over medium-high heat 4 to 5 minutes or until browned. Transfer to a bowl.

3. Cook tomatoes in 1 Tbsp. hot oil in skillet over medium-high heat, stirring occasionally, 2 to 3 minutes or until skins are charred. Place in bowl with okra.

4. Sauté shrimp, garlic, and dried crushed red pepper in remaining 1 Tbsp. hot oil in skillet over medium-high heat 2 to 3 minutes or just until shrimp turn pink. Stir in okra and tomatoes. Season with salt and pepper to taste; cook 1 to 2 minutes or until thoroughly heated.

TASTE OF SUMMER

OKRA

Southerners know all too well the joys of this beloved vegetable. It's available fresh year-round in the South, and elsewhere from May to October. Select smaller, more tender okra pods that are firm, brightly colored, and free of blemishes. Refrigerate up to 3 days in a plastic bag.

spicy mango shrimp

makes: 6 to 8 servings
hands-on time: 35 min.   total time: 35 min., including rice

Coconut-Lime Rice

1½ lb. peeled, large raw
   shrimp
3   Tbsp. olive oil, divided
1   cup chopped green onions
1   cup diced red bell pepper
2   garlic cloves, minced
1   Tbsp. grated fresh ginger
½   to 1 tsp. dried crushed red
   pepper
1   cup chopped fresh mango
¼   cup chopped fresh cilantro
¼   cup soy sauce
2   Tbsp. fresh lime juice

1. Prepare Coconut-Lime Rice.

2. Meanwhile, sauté half of shrimp in 1 Tbsp. hot oil in a large skillet over medium-high heat 2 to 3 minutes or just until shrimp turn pink. Remove shrimp from skillet. Repeat procedure with 1 Tbsp. hot oil and remaining shrimp.

3. Sauté green onions and next 4 ingredients in remaining 1 Tbsp. hot oil over medium-high heat 1 minute. Stir in mango and next 3 ingredients, and cook 1 minute; stir in shrimp. Serve over hot cooked Coconut-Lime Rice.

coconut-lime rice

makes: 6 servings   hands-on time: 10 min.   total time: 35 min.

1   cup light coconut milk
½   tsp. salt
1½ cups uncooked jasmine rice
1   tsp. lime zest
1½ Tbsp. fresh lime juice

1. Bring coconut milk, salt, and 2 cups water to a boil in a saucepan over medium heat. Stir in rice; cover, reduce heat to low, and simmer, stirring occasionally to prevent scorching, 20 to 25 minutes or until liquid is absorbed and rice is tender. Stir in lime zest and juice.

barbecue shrimp *(pictured on opposite page)*

makes: 6 servings   hands-on time: 10 min.   total time: 35 min.

1½ lb. unpeeled jumbo raw shrimp
1 large lemon, cut into wedges
1 (0.7-oz.) envelope Italian dressing mix
½ cup melted butter
½ cup loosely packed fresh flat-leaf parsley

1. Preheat oven to 425°. Place shrimp and lemon in a 13- x 9-inch baking dish. Stir together dressing mix and butter. Pour butter mixture over shrimp, stirring to coat.

2. Bake, covered, at 425° for 25 to 30 minutes or just until shrimp turn pink, stirring once.

3. Remove shrimp mixture from oven, and sprinkle with parsley.

shrimp succotash

makes: 6 servings   hands-on time: 45 min.   total time: 45 min.

2 cups fresh butter beans (about ½ lb.)*
1¼ tsp. kosher salt, divided
1½ lb. peeled and deveined, extra-large raw shrimp
2 Tbsp. olive oil, divided
¼ tsp. freshly ground pepper
1 cup sliced fresh okra
1 small sweet onion, chopped
1 jalapeño pepper, seeded and minced
½ cup diced red bell pepper
2 garlic cloves, minced
1 medium-size heirloom tomato, seeded and diced
1 cup fresh corn kernels (2 ears)
¼ cup chopped fresh basil
1 Tbsp. butter
Salt and freshly ground pepper to taste

1. Rinse, sort, and drain butter beans.

2. Bring butter beans, 1 tsp. salt, and 4 cups water to a boil in a saucepan over medium-high heat. Reduce heat to medium-low, and simmer, stirring occasionally, 35 minutes or until beans are tender; drain.

3. Meanwhile, combine shrimp, 1 Tbsp. oil, ¼ tsp. pepper, and remaining ¼ tsp. salt in a bowl, tossing to coat. Heat a grill pan over medium-high heat; cook shrimp 4 to 5 minutes or just until shrimp turn pink. Transfer to a plate, and cover loosely with aluminum foil to keep warm.

4. Heat remaining 1 Tbsp. oil in a large skillet over medium heat. Add okra; cook 3 minutes or until lightly browned. Stir in onion and next 3 ingredients; cook 3 minutes or until vegetables are tender. Add tomato and corn; sauté 3 to 4 minutes or until corn is tender. Stir in basil, butter, shrimp, and butter beans. Cook 1 minute or until butter is melted and mixture is thoroughly heated. Season with salt and pepper to taste. Serve immediately.

* Frozen butter beans may be substituted. Omit Step 1.

main dishes

195

crunchy crab cakes (pictured on opposite page)

makes: 8 servings   hands-on time: 23 min.   total time: 25 min.

1   (16-oz.) package fresh lump
      crabmeat, drained
4   large lemons, divided
1   (4-oz.) jar diced pimiento, well
      drained
2   green onions, chopped
1   large egg, lightly beaten
2   Tbsp. mayonnaise
1   tsp. Old Bay seasoning
2   tsp. Dijon mustard
1   cup panko (Japanese
      breadcrumbs), divided
¼   cup canola oil
Garnishes: lemon zest, sliced
green onions, sour cream

1. Pick crabmeat, removing any bits of shell.

2. Grate zest from 2 lemons to equal 2 tsp.; cut lemons in half, and squeeze juice into a measuring cup to equal ¼ cup. Stir together lemon zest and juice, pimiento, and next 5 ingredients until well blended. Gently fold in crabmeat and ½ cup breadcrumbs.

3. Shape mixture into 8 patties. Dredge patties in remaining ½ cup breadcrumbs.

4. Cook half of patties in 2 Tbsp. hot oil in a large nonstick skillet over medium heat 2 minutes on each side or until golden brown; drain on a wire rack. Repeat procedure with remaining oil and patties.

5. Cut remaining 2 lemons into wedges. Garnish, if desired.

beer-battered fried fish (pictured on pages 6-7)

makes: 8 servings   hands-on time: 30 min.   total time: 30 min.

Vegetable oil
2   lb. grouper fillets, cut into
      pieces
1   tsp. salt
½   tsp. freshly ground pepper
1½ cups all-purpose flour
1½ tsp. sugar
1   tsp. salt
1   (12-oz.) bottle beer
1   tsp. hot sauce

1. Pour oil to a depth of 3 inches into a large Dutch oven; heat to 360°.

2. Meanwhile, sprinkle fish with salt and pepper.

3. Whisk together flour and next 2 ingredients in a large bowl. Whisk in beer and hot sauce. Dip fish in batter, allowing excess batter to drip off.

4. Gently lower fish into hot oil using tongs (to prevent fish from sticking to Dutch oven). Fry fish, in 4 batches, 2 to 3 minutes on each side or until golden brown. Place fried fish on a wire rack in a jelly-roll pan; keep warm in a 200° oven until ready to serve.

grilled grouper with watermelon salsa

makes: 4 servings   hands-on time: 21 min.   total time: 21 min.

4   (4-oz.) grouper fillets
1   tsp. freshly ground
    black pepper
1   tsp. salt, divided
3   Tbsp. olive oil, divided
2   cups chopped seedless
    watermelon
¼   cup chopped pitted kalamata
    olives
½   English cucumber, chopped
1   small jalapeño pepper, seeded
    and minced
2   Tbsp. minced red onion
2   Tbsp. white balsamic vinegar
Garnish: freshly ground black
    pepper

1. Preheat grill to 350° to 400° (medium-high) heat. Sprinkle grouper with pepper and ½ tsp. salt. Drizzle with 2 Tbsp. olive oil.

2. Grill fish, covered with grill lid, 3 to 4 minutes on each side or just until fish flakes with a fork.

3. Combine chopped watermelon, next 5 ingredients, and remaining ½ tsp. salt and 1 Tbsp. olive oil. Serve with grilled fish. Garnish, if desired.

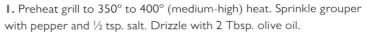

TASTE OF SUMMER

WATERMELON

Watermelon hits its prime in August, sweetening backyard barbecues, lazy-day picnics on the grass, and beach parties. It boasts an unbeatable combination for long, hot days: It's colorful, sweet, crunchy, refreshing, and portable. Choose a firm, symmetrical, unblemished melon with a dull rind, without cracks or soft spots, that barely yields to pressure. Store uncut watermelon at room temperature for up to 1 week. If serving it chilled, refrigerate for 8 to 10 hours.

Roadside Treat

I never, ever want to live anywhere that doesn't have roadside peaches sold at little makeshift stands along the old beach routes. Nothing against the big, swanky interstate peach parks—I shop there, too, happily sampling their ice cream and maybe picking up a hanging basket of petunias or a big bag of peanuts for the road. But I love driving along highways like old U.S. 31, where you can spot the occasional little fruit stand with a tin roof and display tables made of lumber stretched across concrete blocks or saw horses. No flashy signs or gift shops—just rows of garden baskets filled with fresh peaches and tomatoes. Prices will be handwritten on a piece of cardboard tacked onto a post, so you can see it from the highway. A pickup truck covered with dust from the orchards will be parked nearby, and a hound dog might be snoozing in the shade.

I don't know why peaches taste better when you carry them home in a garden basket, but they do. And while I always tell myself that this time, I will make my first peach pie or cobbler or maybe a gallon of homemade peach ice cream, I usually devour them fresh before I have time to even look for a recipe. When there are peaches on the kitchen table, I know it's summertime. And I know what I'm having for breakfast.

VFL

grilled tomato-peach pizza

makes: 4 servings
hands-on time: 26 min.   total time: 26 min.

Vegetable cooking spray
2   tomatoes, sliced
½ tsp. salt
1   large peach, peeled and
    sliced
1   lb. bakery pizza dough

½ (16-oz.) package fresh
    mozzarella, sliced
10 to 12 fresh basil leaves
Garnishes: coarsely ground
    pepper, olive oil

1. Coat cold cooking grate of grill with cooking spray, and place on grill. Preheat grill to 300° to 350° (medium) heat.

2. Sprinkle tomatoes with salt; let stand 15 minutes. Pat tomatoes dry with paper towels.

3. Grill peach slices, covered with grill lid, 2 to 3 minutes on each side or until grill marks appear.

4. Place dough on a large baking sheet coated with cooking spray; lightly coat dough with cooking spray. Roll dough to ¼-inch thickness (about 14 inches in diameter). Slide pizza dough from baking sheet onto cooking grate.

5. Grill, covered with grill lid, 2 to 3 minutes or until lightly browned. Turn dough over, and reduce temperature to 250° to 300° (low) heat; top with tomatoes, grilled peaches, and mozzarella. Grill, covered with grill lid, 5 minutes or until cheese melts. Arrange basil leaves over pizza. Garnish, if desired. Serve immediately.

INDULGENT

sweet tea icebox tart

makes: 12 servings
hands-on time: 25 min.
total time: 5 hr., 52 min., including crust

2   Tbsp. unsweetened instant
    iced tea mix
1   (14-oz.) can sweetened
    condensed milk
½   tsp. orange zest
½   tsp. lime zest
⅓   cup fresh orange juice
¼   cup fresh lemon juice
2   large eggs, lightly beaten
Gingersnap Crust*
1   cup heavy cream
3   Tbsp. sugar
Garnishes: lemon slices, fresh
    mint sprigs, orange slices

1. Preheat oven to 350°. Stir together iced tea mix and 2 Tbsp. water in a large bowl. Whisk in sweetened condensed milk and next 5 ingredients until blended. Place Gingersnap Crust on a baking sheet; pour in milk mixture.

2. Bake at 350° for 20 to 25 minutes or just until filling is set. Cool completely on a wire rack (about 1 hour). Cover and chill 4 to 24 hours. Remove tart from pan, and place on a serving dish.

3. Beat cream and sugar at medium speed with an electric mixer until stiff peaks form. Dollop or pipe on top of tart; garnish, if desired.

*2 (4-oz.) packages ready-made mini graham cracker piecrusts may be substituted.

note: You may also bake this tart in a 14- x 4-inch tart pan with a removable bottom; increase bake time to 25 to 28 minutes or until filling is set.

gingersnap crust

makes: 1 (9-inch) crust
hands-on time: 7 min.   total time: 7 min.

1½ cups crushed gingersnap
    cookies
5   Tbsp. butter, melted
2   Tbsp. light brown sugar
¼   tsp. ground cinnamon

1. Stir together all ingredients. Press mixture into a 9-inch tart pan with removable bottom.

indulgent

MINT

Southern food and beverages just wouldn't be the same without this essential herb—it makes a glass of sweet iced tea just a little more perfect and even a Kentucky Derby wouldn't be complete without it! Bursting with fragrance and color, mint adds dimension to both sweet and savory dishes. It's easy to cultivate, so you can have it on hand to flavor icy beverages, main dish salads and entrées, and stunning sweets. If you're buying mint at the market, look for bright green, crisp leaves with no signs of wilting. Place the stems in a glass containing a couple of inches of water, and cover leaves loosely with plastic wrap or a zip-top plastic bag (do not seal the bag). Refrigerate for up to 1 week, changing the water every other day.

tipsy spiced fruit tart

makes: 8 servings   hands-on time: 35 min.
total time: 2 hr., including whipped cream, plus 24 hr. for chilling

⅔   cup bourbon or brandy
¾   tsp. ground cinnamon
¼   tsp. ground allspice
¾   cup granulated sugar, divided
1   cup halved dried Mission figlets
1   (7-oz.) package dried apricots, coarsely chopped
1   cup jumbo raisins
3   ripe Bartlett pears, peeled and chopped
2   Tbsp. all-purpose flour
2   tsp. finely grated fresh ginger
1   (14.1-oz.) package refrigerated piecrusts
Parchment paper
1   large egg, beaten
2   tsp. Demerara sugar*
Buttermilk Whipped Cream (optional)

1. Cook bourbon, next 2 ingredients, and ½ cup granulated sugar in a medium saucepan over medium-low heat, stirring often, 3 minutes or until sugar dissolves and mixture is hot. Remove from heat, and stir in figlets, apricots, and raisins. Pour mixture into a large zip-top plastic freezer bag. Seal bag, removing as much air as possible; chill 24 hours.

2. Preheat oven to 350°. Transfer fruit mixture to a large bowl; stir in pears, flour, ginger, and remaining ¼ cup sugar.

3. Unroll and stack piecrusts on parchment paper. Roll into a 12-inch circle. Mound fruit mixture in center of piecrust (mixture will be slightly runny), leaving a 2- to 2½-inch border. Fold piecrust border up and over fruit, pleating as you go, leaving an opening about 5 inches wide in center. Brush piecrust with egg, and sprinkle with 2 tsp. Demerara sugar. Slide parchment paper onto a baking sheet.

4. Bake at 350° for 50 minutes or until filling is bubbly and crust is golden brown. Cool on baking sheet on a wire rack 30 minutes. Serve warm or at room temperature with Buttermilk Whipped Cream, if desired.

*Granulated sugar may be substituted.

note: We tested with Sun-Maid Mediterranean Apricots.

buttermilk whipped cream

Freeze the bowl and beaters, and use cream and buttermilk right out of the fridge for perfect results.

makes: 3 cups   hands-on time: 5 min.   total time: 5 min.

1   cup heavy cream
½   cup buttermilk
2   Tbsp. sugar

1. Beat first 2 ingredients at high speed with an electric mixer until foamy; gradually add sugar, beating until soft peaks form. Serve immediately, or cover and chill for up to 2 hours.

SIT A SPELL
The Call for Brandy

Fruitcake season always puts my mother in a quandary. The only recipe she will allow is Great-Aunt Margaret's, who believed in soaking her cakes in peach brandy. But Mama is a good Baptist. Drinking's a sin. On the other hand, ruining a treasured recipe has got to be nigh unto one. So she compromises. She uses the brandy, but she sends for it. There for a while, my cousin Eddie would be dispatched to the liquor store in Childersburg every couple of years, with instructions to deliver the brandy to Mama's back door, preferably under cloak of darkness. When Eddie moved South, my husband and I started getting the call. Last time, Mama said her supply had depleted far too quickly. She suspected Daddy was "slippin' and sippin'." For his part, Daddy vehemently denies all allegations. He's going with the "probably just evaporated" defense.

VFL

chocolate-pecan chess pie

Dark, rich, and intensely chocolaty, this is our favorite new twist on pecan pie.

makes: 8 servings
hands-on time: 15 min.   total time: 2 hr., 15 min.

½ (14.1-oz.) package refrigerated piecrusts
½ cup butter
2 (1-oz.) unsweetened chocolate baking squares
1 (5-oz.) can evaporated milk (⅔ cup)
2 large eggs
2 tsp. vanilla extract, divided
1½ cups granulated sugar
3 Tbsp. unsweetened cocoa
2 Tbsp. all-purpose flour
⅛ tsp. salt
1½ cups pecan halves and pieces
⅔ cup firmly packed light brown sugar
1 Tbsp. light corn syrup

1. Preheat oven to 350°. Roll piecrust into a 13-inch circle on a lightly floured surface. Fit into a 9-inch pie plate; fold edges under, and crimp.

2. Microwave butter and chocolate squares in a large microwave-safe bowl at MEDIUM (50% power) 1½ minutes or until melted and smooth, stirring at 30-second intervals. Whisk in evaporated milk, eggs, and 1 tsp. vanilla.

3. Stir together granulated sugar and next 3 ingredients. Add sugar mixture to chocolate mixture, whisking until smooth. Pour mixture into prepared crust.

4. Bake pie at 350° for 40 minutes. Stir together pecans, next 2 ingredients, and remaining 1 tsp. vanilla; sprinkle over pie. Bake 10 more minutes or until set. Remove from oven to a wire rack, and cool completely (about 1 hour).

Y'ALL ENJOY

Comfort Food Menu

4 servings

Hamburger Steak with Sweet Onion-Mushroom Gravy *(page 77)*

Mashed potatoes

Green Beans with Roasted Tomatoes *(page 269)*

Jordan Rolls *(page 250)*

Tangerine Chess Pie

---

tangerine chess pie (pictured on opposite page, top left)

makes: 6 to 8 servings
hands-on time: 15 min.   total time: 2 hr., 18 min.

1   (14.1-oz.) package refrigerated piecrusts
1½ cups sugar
1   Tbsp. all-purpose flour
1   Tbsp. plain yellow cornmeal
¼   tsp. salt
¼   cup butter, melted
2   tsp. tangerine or orange zest
⅓   cup fresh tangerine or orange juice
1   Tbsp. lemon juice
4   large eggs, lightly beaten
Garnishes: sweetened whipped cream, tangerine slices, tangerine zest

1. Preheat oven to 450°. Unroll piecrusts; stack on a lightly floured surface. Roll into a 12-inch circle. Fit piecrust into a 9-inch pie plate; fold edges under, and crimp. Prick bottom and sides of crust with a fork. Bake 8 minutes; cool on a wire rack 15 minutes. Reduce oven temperature to 350°.

2. Whisk together sugar and next 8 ingredients until blended. Pour into prepared piecrust.

3. Bake at 350° for 40 to 45 minutes or until center is set, shielding edges with foil after 20 minutes to prevent excessive browning. Cool 1 hour. Garnish, if desired.

easy skillet apple pie

makes: 8 to 10 servings
hands-on time: 20 min.   total time: 1 hr., 50 min.

2   lb. Granny Smith apples
2   lb. Braeburn apples
1   tsp. ground cinnamon
¾   cup granulated sugar
½   cup butter
1   cup firmly packed light brown
    sugar
1   (14.1-oz.) package refrigerated
    piecrusts
1   egg white
2   Tbsp. granulated sugar

1. Preheat oven to 350°. Peel apples, and cut into ½-inch-thick wedges. Toss apples with cinnamon and ¾ cup granulated sugar.

2. Melt butter in a 10-inch cast-iron skillet over medium heat; add brown sugar, and cook, stirring constantly, 1 to 2 minutes or until sugar dissolves. Remove from heat, and place 1 piecrust in skillet over brown sugar mixture. Spoon apple mixture over piecrust, and top with remaining piecrust. Whisk egg white until foamy. Brush top of piecrust with egg white; sprinkle with 2 Tbsp. granulated sugar. Cut 4 or 5 slits in top for steam to escape.

3. Bake at 350° for 1 hour to 1 hour and 10 minutes or until golden brown and bubbly, shielding with aluminum foil during last 10 minutes to prevent excessive browning, if necessary. Cool on a wire rack 30 minutes before serving.

TASTE OF WINTER

APPLES

Fall's favorite fruit shows up in some sinfully delicious temptations from apple pies to apple cakes. Apples are available year-round, but they're best from September to November. Look for firm, vibrantly colored apples with no bruises. They should smell fresh, not musty. Skins should be tight and smooth. Though you may be tempted to display apples in a fruit bowl, resist the urge. Store them in a plastic bag in the refrigerator for up to 6 weeks. The plastic bag will prevent them from accelerating the ripening of other produce in your refrigerator.

apple-cherry cobbler with pinwheel biscuits

makes: 8 to 10 servings
hands-on time: 1 hr.   total time: 1 hr., 15 min.

Apple-Cherry Filling:

8   large Braeburn apples,
     peeled and cut into
     ½-inch-thick wedges
     (about 4½ lb.)
2   cups granulated sugar
¼   cup all-purpose flour
¼   cup butter
1   (12-oz.) package frozen
     cherries, thawed and well
     drained
1   tsp. lemon zest
⅓   cup fresh lemon juice
1   tsp. ground cinnamon

Pinwheel Biscuits:

2¼ cups all-purpose flour
¼   cup granulated sugar
2¼ tsp. baking powder
¾   tsp. salt
¾   cup cold butter, cut into
     pieces
⅔   cup milk
⅔   cup firmly packed light
     brown sugar
2   Tbsp. butter, melted
¼   cup finely chopped
     roasted unsalted almonds
Garnish: sweetened whipped
     cream

1. Prepare Filling: Preheat oven to 425°. Toss together first
3 ingredients. Melt ¼ cup butter in a large skillet over medium-high
heat; add apple mixture. Cook, stirring often, 20 to 25 minutes
or until apples are tender and syrup thickens. Remove from heat;
stir in cherries and next 3 ingredients. Spoon apple mixture into a
lightly greased 3-qt. baking dish. Bake 12 minutes, placing a baking
sheet on oven rack directly below baking dish to catch any drips.

2. Prepare Biscuits: Stir together 2¼ cups flour and next 3 ingredients. Cut cold butter pieces into mixture with a pastry blender or
fork until crumbly; stir in milk. Turn dough out onto a lightly floured
surface; knead 4 or 5 times. Roll dough into a 12-inch square. Combine brown sugar and 2 Tbsp. melted butter; sprinkle over dough,
patting gently. Sprinkle with almonds. Roll up, jelly-roll fashion; pinch
seams and ends to seal. Cut roll into 12 (1-inch) slices. Place slices
in a single layer on top of apple mixture. Bake at 425° for 15 to
17 minutes or until biscuits are golden. Garnish, if desired.

Miss Jackie's Biscuits

My mother is a wonderful cook, but she never mastered biscuits. As a child, I thought all biscuits came from a can. But then my friend Sarah invited me for a sleepover, and I got to watch, spellbound, as her mother made a little well of milk in a bowl of flour and worked the ingredients together with her hand. She would roll the dough into little balls and press her knuckle into each one to make an imprint. As the biscuits baked, the imprints disappeared, leaving behind golden clouds of goodness. Breakfast at Sarah's house always included scrambled eggs and sausage with those amazing biscuits—and ice-cold Coca-Cola. (Her daddy believed in keeping plenty of Cokes in the refrigerator, and we girls reaped the benefits.) What I remember most about those mornings is the way Sarah's mother always made me feel so at home. Every time I have a truly great biscuit, I think of her and remember those weekend visits from my childhood, when I would fall asleep giggling with my dear friend and wake up to the tantalizing aroma of the best biscuits I ever had.

VFL

SIT A SPELL

Creole bread pudding with bourbon sauce

makes: 10 to 12 servings
hands-on time: 20 min.
total time: 1 hr., 15 min., including sauce

2   (12-oz.) cans evaporated milk
6   large eggs, lightly beaten
1   (16-oz.) day-old French bread loaf, cubed
1   (8-oz.) can crushed pineapple, drained
1   large Red Delicious apple, unpeeled and grated
1½ cups sugar
1   cup raisins
5   Tbsp. vanilla extract
¼   cup butter, cut into ½-inch cubes and softened
Bourbon Sauce

1. Preheat oven to 350°. Whisk together evaporated milk, eggs, and 1 cup water in a large bowl until well blended. Add bread cubes, stirring to coat thoroughly. Stir in pineapple and next 4 ingredients. Stir in butter, blending well. Pour into a greased 13- x 9-inch baking dish.

2. Bake at 350° for 35 to 45 minutes or until set and crust is golden. Remove from oven, and let stand 2 minutes. Serve with Bourbon Sauce.

bourbon sauce

makes: 1½ cups   hands-on time: 18 min.   total time: 18 min.

3   Tbsp. butter
1   Tbsp. all-purpose flour
1   cup whipping cream
½   cup sugar
2   Tbsp. bourbon
1   Tbsp. vanilla extract
1   tsp. ground nutmeg

1. Melt butter in a small saucepan over medium-low heat; whisk in flour, and cook, whisking constantly, 5 minutes. Stir in cream and sugar; cook, whisking constantly, 3 minutes or until thickened. Stir in bourbon, vanilla, and nutmeg; cook, whisking constantly, 5 minutes or until thoroughly heated.

peanut butter-banana-sandwich bread puddings with dark caramel sauce

makes: 8 servings
hands-on time: 25 min.
total time: 3 hr., 56 min., including topping and sauce

8 buttermilk bread slices, crusts removed
½ cup creamy peanut butter
2 bananas, thinly sliced
2 large eggs
½ cup granulated sugar
2 Tbsp. brown sugar
1¾ cups whipping cream
Peanut Butter Streusel Topping
Dark Caramel Sauce
Garnish: whipped cream

1. Spread bread slices with peanut butter. Top 4 bread slices with bananas and remaining bread slices, peanut butter sides down, pressing firmly. Cut sandwiches into 1-inch pieces; place in 8 lightly greased (8-oz.) ramekins.

2. Whisk together eggs and sugars; whisk in whipping cream. Gradually pour mixture over sandwich pieces in ramekins; sprinkle with Peanut Butter Streusel Topping. Place ramekins in a 15- x 10-inch jelly-roll pan. Cover and chill 2 to 24 hours.

3. Preheat oven to 375°. Let puddings stand at room temperature 30 minutes. Bake at 375° for 20 to 25 minutes or until golden, set, and puffed. Serve warm with caramel sauce. Garnish, if desired.

peanut butter streusel topping

makes: 1 cup   hands-on time: 10 min.   total time: 10 min.

¼ cup all-purpose flour
¼ cup firmly packed brown sugar
2 Tbsp. butter
2 Tbsp. creamy peanut butter
¼ cup chopped salted peanuts

1. Stir together flour and brown sugar in a bowl. Cut in butter and peanut butter with pastry blender or fork until mixture resembles small peas. Stir in peanuts.

dark caramel sauce

makes: 1½ cups   hands-on time: 16 min.   total time: 31 min.

1 cup sugar
1 cup whipping cream
1 tsp. vanilla extract
⅛ to ¼ tsp. salt

1. Cook sugar in a 3-qt. heavy saucepan over medium heat 6 to 8 minutes or until sugar caramelizes, swirling pan to incorporate mixture. Stir in whipping cream. (Mixture will bubble and harden.) Cook, stirring constantly, until mixture melts and begins to boil (about 5 minutes). Quickly pour sauce into a bowl; stir in vanilla and salt. Cool 15 minutes.

nutter butter® banana pudding trifle

makes: 8 to 10 servings
hands-on time: 55 min.   total time: 3 hr., 25 min.

3   cups milk
3   large eggs
¾   cup sugar
⅓   cup all-purpose flour
2   Tbsp. butter
2   tsp. vanilla extract
5   medium-size ripe bananas
1   (1-lb.) package peanut butter
     sandwich cookies
2   cups sweetened whipped
     cream
Garnishes: peanut butter sandwich
     cookies, banana slices

1. Whisk together first 4 ingredients in a large saucepan over medium-low heat. Cook, whisking constantly, 15 to 20 minutes or until thickened. Remove from heat; stir in butter and vanilla until butter melts.

2. Fill a large bowl with ice. Place saucepan in ice, and let stand, stirring occasionally, 30 minutes or until mixture is thoroughly chilled.

3. Meanwhile, cut bananas into ¼-inch slices. Break cookies into thirds.

4. Spoon half of pudding mixture into a 3-qt. bowl or pitcher, or divide between 2 (1½- to 2-qt.) widemouthed pitchers. Top with bananas and cookies. Spoon remaining pudding mixture over bananas and cookies. Top with sweetened whipped cream. Cover and chill 2 to 24 hours. Garnish, if desired.

note: We tested with Nabisco Nutter Butter® Sandwich Cookies.

Try This Twist!

shortcut nutter butter®-banana pudding trifle: Omit eggs, sugar, flour, and butter. Substitute thawed extra creamy whipped topping for sweetened whipped cream. Reduce vanilla to 1 tsp. Place 3 cups milk and vanilla in large bowl; add 2 (3.4-oz.) packages vanilla instant pudding mix. Beat at medium speed with an electric mixer 2 minutes or until thickened; let stand 5 minutes. Stir in 1 (8-oz.) container sour cream. Proceed with recipe as directed in Steps 2 through 4.

note: We tested with Jell-O Vanilla Instant Pudding and Pie Filling and Cool Whip Extra Creamy.

desserts

Y'ALL ENJOY

Sweet Soirée

10 to 12 servings

Sweet Tea Tiramisù

Mississippi Mud Cake *(page 228)*

Strawberry-Lemon Shortbread Bars *(page 239)*

Buttermilk Pound Cake with Buttermilk Custard Sauce *(page 226)*

---

sweet tea tiramisù *(pictured on opposite page, top left)*

makes: 10 to 12 servings
hands-on time: 20 min.   total time: 13 hr., 30 min.

2   family-size tea bags
1½ cups sugar, divided
2   (8-oz.) containers mascarpone
      cheese
1   Tbsp. vanilla bean paste
      or vanilla extract
2   cups whipping cream
2   (3-oz.) packages ladyfingers

1. Bring 4 cups water to a boil in a 3-qt. heavy saucepan; add tea bags. Remove from heat; cover and steep 10 minutes.

2. Discard tea bags. Add 1 cup sugar, stirring until dissolved. Bring tea mixture to a boil over medium-high heat, and cook, stirring occasionally, 20 to 22 minutes or until mixture is reduced to 1 cup. Remove mixture from heat, and cool to room temperature (about 30 minutes).

3. Stir together mascarpone cheese, vanilla bean paste, and remaining ½ cup sugar.

4. Beat whipping cream at medium speed with an electric mixer until soft peaks form; fold into cheese mixture.

5. Separate ladyfingers in half. Arrange 24 ladyfinger halves, flat sides up, in the bottom of an 11- x 7-inch baking dish. Drizzle with half of tea mixture. Top with half of cheese mixture. Repeat layers once. Cover and chill 12 hours.

strawberry semifreddo shortcake

Marshmallow crème stirred into this shortcake eliminates the traditional use for raw eggs. Ladyfingers make a pretty and tasty crust for this divine dessert. Look for soft ladyfingers in the bakery section of the grocery store.

makes: 16 servings
hands-on time: 30 min.   total time: 5 hr., 45 min.

2 (3-oz.) packages soft ladyfingers
2 pt. strawberry ice cream, softened
1 pt. strawberry sorbet, softened
1 pt. fresh strawberries, hulled
2 Tbsp. powdered sugar
½ (7-oz.) jar marshmallow crème
1 cup heavy cream

1. Arrange ladyfingers around sides and on bottom of a 9-inch springform pan. (Reserve any remaining ladyfingers for another use.) Spread strawberry ice cream over ladyfingers, and freeze 30 minutes.

2. Spread softened strawberry sorbet over ice cream. Freeze 30 minutes.

3. Process strawberries and powdered sugar in a food processor 1 minute or until pureed. Reserve ¼ cup mixture. Whisk remaining strawberry mixture into marshmallow crème until well blended.

4. Beat cream at high speed with an electric mixer until stiff peaks form. Fold into marshmallow mixture. Pour over sorbet in pan. Drizzle reserved strawberry mixture over top, and gently swirl with a paring knife. Freeze 4 hours or until firm. Let cake stand at room temperature 15 minutes before serving.

note: We tested with Blue Bell Strawberry Ice Cream and Häagen-Dazs Strawberry Sorbet.

buttermilk pound cake with buttermilk custard sauce

makes: 12 servings
hands-on time: 15 min.
total time: 2 hr., 45 min., including sauce

1⅓ cups butter, softened
2½ cups sugar
6 large eggs
3 cups all-purpose flour
½ cup buttermilk
1 tsp. vanilla extract
Buttermilk Custard Sauce
Garnishes: blueberries,
    raspberries, mint sprigs

1. Preheat oven to 325°. Beat butter at medium speed with a heavy-duty electric stand mixer until creamy. Gradually add sugar, beating at medium speed until light and fluffy. Add eggs, 1 at a time, beating just until blended after each addition.

2. Add flour to butter mixture alternately with buttermilk, beginning and ending with flour. Beat at low speed just until blended after each addition. Stir in vanilla. Pour batter into a greased and floured 10-inch (12-cup) tube pan.

3. Bake at 325° for 1 hour and 5 minutes to 1 hour and 10 minutes or until a long wooden pick inserted in center comes out clean. Cool in pan on a wire rack 10 to 15 minutes; remove from pan to wire rack, and cool completely (about 1 hour). Serve with Buttermilk Custard Sauce. Garnish, if desired.

buttermilk custard sauce

makes: about 2⅓ cups
hands-on time: 15 min.   total time: 15 min.

2 cups buttermilk
½ cup sugar
1 Tbsp. cornstarch
3 egg yolks
1 tsp. vanilla extract

1. Whisk together buttermilk, sugar, cornstarch, and egg yolks in a heavy 3-qt. saucepan. Bring to a boil over medium heat, whisking constantly, and boil 1 minute. Remove from heat, and stir in vanilla. Serve warm or cold. Store leftovers in an airtight container in refrigerator for up to 1 week.

Mississippi mud cake

makes: 15 servings
hands-on time: 15 min.   total time: 40 min.

1   cup chopped pecans
1   cup butter
4   oz. semisweet chocolate, chopped
2   cups sugar
1½ cups all-purpose flour
½   cup unsweetened cocoa
4   large eggs
1   tsp. vanilla extract
¾   tsp. salt
1   (10.5-oz.) bag miniature marshmallows
Chocolate Frosting

1. Preheat oven to 350°. Place pecans in a single layer on a baking sheet. Bake at 350° for 8 to 10 minutes or until toasted, stirring halfway through. Microwave 1 cup butter and semisweet chocolate in a large microwave-safe glass bowl at HIGH 1 minute or until melted and smooth, stirring at 30-second intervals.

2. Whisk sugar and next 5 ingredients into chocolate mixture. Pour batter into a greased 15- x 10-inch jelly-roll pan. Bake at 350° for 20 minutes. Remove from oven, and sprinkle with miniature marshmallows; bake 8 to 10 more minutes or until golden brown. Drizzle warm cake with Chocolate Frosting, and sprinkle with toasted pecans.

chocolate frosting

makes: about 2 cups
hands-on time: 10 min.   total time: 15 min.

½   cup butter
⅓   cup unsweetened cocoa
⅓   cup milk
1   (16-oz.) package powdered sugar
1   tsp. vanilla extract

1. Stir together first 3 ingredients in a medium saucepan over medium heat until butter melts. Cook, stirring constantly, 2 minutes or until slightly thickened; remove from heat. Beat in powdered sugar and 1 tsp. vanilla at medium-high speed with an electric mixer until smooth.

Try This Twist!

Mississippi mud cupcakes: Prepare pecans and Mississippi Mud Cake batter as directed. Spoon into 24 paper-lined muffin cups. Bake at 350° for 20 minutes or until puffed. Sprinkle with 2 cups miniature marshmallows; bake 5 more minutes or until a wooden pick inserted in center comes out clean. Remove from oven; cool in muffin pans 5 minutes. Remove from pans; place on wire rack. Drizzle warm cakes with 1¼ cups Chocolate Frosting; sprinkle with pecans.

desserts

hummingbird Bundt cake

makes: 10 to 12 servings
hands-on time: 10 min.
total time: 3 hr., 45 min., including glaze

1½ cups chopped pecans
3   cups all-purpose flour
2   cups sugar
1   tsp. baking soda
1   tsp. ground cinnamon
½   tsp. salt
3   large eggs, lightly beaten
1¾ cups mashed ripe bananas
     (about 4 large)
1   (8-oz.) can crushed pineapple,
     undrained
¾   cup canola oil
1½ tsp. vanilla extract
Glaze

1. Preheat oven to 350°. Bake pecans in a single layer in a shallow pan 8 to 10 minutes or until toasted and fragrant, stirring halfway through.

2. Stir together flour and next 4 ingredients in a large bowl; stir in eggs and next 4 ingredients, stirring just until dry ingredients are moistened. Sprinkle 1 cup toasted pecans into a greased and floured 14-cup Bundt pan. Spoon batter over pecans.

3. Bake at 350° for 1 hour to 1 hour and 10 minutes or until a long wooden pick inserted in center comes out clean. Cool cake in pan on a wire rack 15 minutes; remove from pan to wire rack, and cool completely (about 2 hours).

4. When cake has cooled, make glaze. Immediately pour glaze over cooled cake, and sprinkle with remaining ½ cup toasted pecans.

glaze

4   oz. cream cheese, cubed and
     softened
2   cups sifted powdered sugar
1   tsp. vanilla extract
1   to 2 Tbsp. milk

1. Process cream cheese, powdered sugar, vanilla, and 1 Tbsp. milk in a food processor until well blended. Add remaining 1 Tbsp. milk, 1 tsp. at a time, processing until smooth.

peach melba shortcakes

makes: 8 servings
hands-on time: 20 min.
total time: 45 min., including whipped cream

2½ cups all-purpose flour
1   Tbsp. plus 1 tsp. baking
    powder
1   tsp. salt
7   Tbsp. sugar, divided
¼   cup cold butter, cut into small
    cubes
1   large egg
½   tsp. vanilla extract
¾   cup half-and-half
Parchment paper
1   Tbsp. half-and-half
6   large fresh, ripe peaches,
    peeled and sliced
1   Tbsp. fresh lemon juice
1½ tsp. vanilla bean paste
2   pt. fresh raspberries
¼   cup honey
Sorghum Whipped Cream

1. Preheat oven to 425°. Combine first 3 ingredients and 1 Tbsp. sugar in a large bowl; cut in butter with a pastry blender or fork until crumbly. Whisk together egg, vanilla, and ¾ cup half-and-half; add to dry ingredients, stirring just until dry ingredients are moistened and dough comes together.

2. Turn dough out onto a lightly floured surface; roll or pat dough into a 7-inch circle (about 1 inch thick). Cut into 8 wedges; place on a parchment paper-lined baking sheet. Brush tops with 1 Tbsp. half-and-half; sprinkle with 2 Tbsp. sugar.

3. Bake at 425° for 15 to 20 minutes or until golden.

4. Meanwhile, stir together peaches, next 2 ingredients, and remaining 4 Tbsp. sugar in a bowl.

5. Cook raspberries and honey in a medium saucepan over medium-low heat 3 minutes, stirring with a fork to lightly crush berries. Spoon raspberry mixture onto 8 individual serving plates.

6. Split warm shortcakes in half horizontally. Place shortcake bottoms on top of raspberry mixture, and top with peaches, Sorghum Whipped Cream, and shortcake tops.

sorghum whipped cream

makes: about 2 cups   hands-on time: 5 min.   total time: 5 min.

1   cup whipping cream
2   Tbsp. sorghum syrup

1. Beat whipping cream at high speed with an electric mixer until foamy; add sorghum syrup, and beat until soft peaks form.

sweet potato cupcakes with cream cheese frosting

makes: 2 dozen
hands-on time: 15 min.   total time: 1 hr., 55 min.

1   cup coarsely chopped pecans
2   cups sugar
1   cup butter, softened
4   large eggs
1   (16-oz.) can mashed sweet potatoes
⅔   cup orange juice
1   tsp. vanilla extract
3   cups all-purpose flour
1   tsp. baking powder
1   tsp. ground cinnamon
½   tsp. baking soda
½   tsp. ground nutmeg
¼   tsp. salt
24 paper baking cups
Vegetable cooking spray
Cream Cheese Frosting
Garnish: coarsely chopped pecans

1. Preheat oven to 350°. Place pecans in a single layer in a shallow pan.

2. Bake at 350° for 8 to 10 minutes or until toasted, stirring halfway through.

3. Beat sugar and butter at medium speed with an electric mixer until blended. Add eggs, 1 at a time, beating until blended after each addition.

4. Whisk together mashed sweet potatoes, orange juice, and vanilla. Combine flour and next 5 ingredients. Add flour mixture to sugar mixture alternately with sweet potato mixture, beginning and ending with flour mixture. Beat at low speed just until blended after each addition. Fold in toasted pecans. Place baking cups in muffin pans, and coat with cooking spray; spoon batter into cups, filling two-thirds full.

5. Bake at 350° for 28 to 30 minutes or until a wooden pick inserted in center comes out clean. Remove immediately from pans, and cool 50 minutes to 1 hour or until completely cool. Spread cupcakes evenly with Cream Cheese Frosting. Garnish, if desired.

cream cheese frosting

makes: 3½ cups   hands-on time: 5 min.   total time: 5 min.

1   (8-oz.) package cream cheese, softened
½   cup butter, softened
1   (16-oz.) package powdered sugar, sifted
1   tsp. vanilla extract

1. Beat cream cheese and butter until fluffy. Gradually add powdered sugar, beating at low speed until blended; add vanilla, beating until blended.

caramel-apple cheesecake

makes: 12 servings
hands-on time: 30 min.   total time: 12 hr., 5 min.

2¾ lb. large Granny Smith apples
   (about 6 apples)
1⅔ cups firmly packed light brown
   sugar, divided
1   Tbsp. butter
2   cups cinnamon graham cracker
   crumbs (about 15 whole
   crackers)
½   cup melted butter
½   cup finely chopped pecans
3   (8-oz.) packages cream cheese,
   softened
2   tsp. vanilla extract
3   large eggs
¼   cup apple jelly

1. Peel apples, and cut into ½-inch-thick wedges. Toss together apples and ⅓ cup brown sugar. Melt 1 Tbsp. butter in a large skillet over medium-high heat; add apple mixture, and sauté 5 to 6 minutes or until crisp-tender and golden. Cool completely (about 30 minutes).

2. Meanwhile, preheat oven to 350°. Stir together cinnamon graham cracker crumbs and next 2 ingredients in a medium bowl until well blended. Press mixture on bottom and 1½ inches up sides of a 9-inch springform pan. Bake 10 to 12 minutes or until lightly browned. Remove to a wire rack, and cool crust completely before filling (about 30 minutes).

3. Beat cream cheese, vanilla, and remaining 1⅓ cups brown sugar at medium speed with a heavy-duty electric stand mixer until blended and smooth. Add eggs, 1 at a time, beating just until blended after each addition. Pour batter into prepared crust. Arrange apples over cream cheese mixture.

4. Bake at 350° for 55 minutes to 1 hour and 5 minutes or until set. Remove from oven, and gently run a knife around outer edge of cheesecake to loosen from sides of pan. (Do not remove sides of pan.) Cool completely on a wire rack (about 2 hours). Cover and chill 8 to 24 hours.

5. Cook apple jelly and 1 tsp. water in a small saucepan over medium heat, stirring constantly, 2 to 3 minutes or until jelly melts; brush over apples on top of cheesecake.

STRAWBERRIES

You know that spring is here when you take that first bite into a plump, juicy strawberry. Enjoy the berries while you can—the season peaks in May.

Choose brightly colored berries that still have their green caps attached. If fully ripe, they should have a potent strawberry fragrance. Store (in a single layer if possible) in a moisture-proof container in the refrigerator for up to 3 or 4 days. Do not rinse the strawberries or remove the hulls until you're ready to use the strawberries. Use an egg slicer to cut strawberries into uniform slices to use in a recipe or for garnish.

strawberry-lemon shortbread bars

Bar cookies go glam in this sweet-tart shortbread bar treat. Cut the bars into single-serving size, and top with a dollop of whipped cream and a sliced strawberry for a top-notch presentation.

makes: 4 dozen
hands-on time: 20 min.   total time: 6 hr., 8 min.

2   cups all-purpose flour
½   cup powdered sugar
¾   tsp. lemon zest, divided
¾   cup cold butter
2   (8-oz.) packages cream
      cheese, softened
¾   cup granulated sugar
2   large eggs
1   Tbsp. fresh lemon juice
1   cup strawberry preserves
Garnishes: sweetened
      whipped cream, fresh
      strawberry slices

1. Preheat oven to 350°. Stir together flour, powdered sugar, and ½ tsp. lemon zest in a medium bowl; cut in butter with a pastry blender until crumbly. Press mixture onto bottom of a lightly greased 13- x 9-inch pan.

2. Bake at 350° for 20 to 22 minutes or until lightly browned.

3. Meanwhile, beat cream cheese and granulated sugar at medium speed with an electric mixer until smooth. Add eggs, 1 at a time, and beat just until blended after each addition. Stir in fresh lemon juice and remaining ¼ tsp. lemon zest, beating well.

4. Spread preserves over shortbread. Pour cream cheese mixture over preserves, spreading to edges. Bake 28 to 32 minutes or until set. Cool 1 hour on a wire rack. Cover and chill 4 to 8 hours. Cut into bars; garnish, if desired.

note: Refrigerate leftovers. Store them in an airtight container for up to 2 days.

swoon pies

makes: 1 dozen
hands-on time: 45 min.   total time: 2 hr., 40 min.

1   cup all-purpose flour
½   tsp. baking powder
½   tsp. baking soda
½   tsp. salt
1   cup graham cracker crumbs
½   cup butter, softened
½   cup granulated sugar
½   cup firmly packed light brown
     sugar
1   large egg
1   tsp. vanilla extract
1   (8-oz.) container sour cream
Parchment paper
Marshmallow Filling
1   (12-oz.) package semisweet
     chocolate morsels
2   tsp. shortening
Toppings: chopped roasted salted
     pecans, chopped crystallized
     ginger, sea salt

1. Preheat oven to 350°. Sift together flour and next 3 ingredients in a medium bowl; stir in graham cracker crumbs. Beat butter and next 2 ingredients at medium speed with a heavy-duty electric stand mixer until fluffy. Add egg and vanilla, beating until blended.

2. Add flour mixture to butter mixture alternately with sour cream, beginning and ending with flour mixture. Beat at low speed until blended after each addition, stopping to scrape bowl as needed. Drop batter by rounded tablespoonfuls 2 inches apart onto 2 parchment paper-lined baking sheets. Bake, in batches, at 350° for 13 to 15 minutes or until set and bottoms are golden brown. Remove cookies (on parchment paper) to wire racks, and cool completely (about 30 minutes).

3. Turn 12 cookies over, flat sides up. Spread each with 1 heaping table-spoonful Marshmallow Filling. Top with remaining 12 cookies, flat sides down, and press gently to spread filling to edges. Freeze on a parchment paper-lined baking sheet 30 minutes or until filling is set.

4. Pour water to depth of 1 inch into a medium saucepan over medium heat; bring to a boil. Reduce heat, and simmer; place chocolate and shortening in a medium-size heatproof bowl over simmering water. Cook, stirring occasionally, 5 to 6 minutes or until melted. Remove from heat, and cool 10 minutes. Meanwhile, remove cookies from freezer, and let stand 10 minutes. Dip half of each cookie sandwich into melted chocolate, allowing excess to drip off. Place on parchment paper-lined baking sheet. Sprinkle with desired topping; freeze 10 minutes or until chocolate is set.

marshmallow filling

makes: about 1½ cups
hands-on time: 5 min.   total time: 5 min.

½   cup butter, softened
1   cup sifted powdered sugar
1   cup marshmallow crème
½   tsp. vanilla extract

1. Beat butter at medium speed with an electric mixer until creamy; gradually add sugar, beating well. Add remaining ingredients, beating until well blended.

peanut butter streusel brownies (pictured at right)

makes: 16 servings
hands-on time: 10 min.   total time: 2 hr.

4   (1-oz.) unsweetened chocolate baking squares
¾   cup butter
1½ cups granulated sugar
½   cup firmly packed brown sugar
3   large eggs
1   cup all-purpose flour

1   tsp. vanilla extract
⅛   tsp. salt
½   cup all-purpose flour
2   Tbsp. granulated sugar
2   Tbsp. light brown sugar
⅓   cup chunky peanut butter
2   Tbsp. melted butter
⅛   tsp. salt

1. Preheat oven to 350°. Line bottom and sides of an 8-inch pan with aluminum foil, allowing 2 to 3 inches to extend over sides; lightly grease foil.

2. Microwave chocolate squares and ¾ cup butter in a large microwave-safe bowl at HIGH 1½ to 2 minutes or until melted and smooth, stirring at 30-second intervals. Whisk in 1½ cups granulated and ½ cup brown sugars. Add eggs, 1 at a time, whisking just until blended after each addition. Whisk in 1 cup flour, vanilla, and ⅛ tsp. salt. Pour mixture into prepared pan.

3. Stir together ½ cup flour, 2 Tbsp. granulated sugar, 2 Tbsp. brown sugar, peanut butter, 2 Tbsp. melted butter, and ⅛ tsp. salt until blended and crumbly. Sprinkle peanut butter mixture over batter.

4. Bake at 350° for 50 to 54 minutes or until a wooden pick inserted in center comes out with a few moist crumbs. Cool completely on a wire rack (about 1 hour). Lift brownies from pan, using foil sides as handles. Gently remove foil, and cut brownies into 16 squares.

thumbprint cookies (pictured at left)

These cookies have a bit of crunch from the finely chopped pecans, sweetness from the almond extract, and richness from the butter. But it's the thumbprint impressions on top that give them a personal touch.

makes: 3½ dozen
hands-on time: 35 min.   total time: 2 hr.

1	cup butter, softened	¼	tsp. salt
¾	cup sugar	1¼	cups finely chopped
2	large eggs, separated		pecans
1	tsp. almond extract	¼	cup strawberry jam
2	cups all-purpose flour	¼	cup peach jam

1. Beat butter at medium speed with an electric mixer until creamy; gradually add sugar, beating well. Add egg yolks and almond extract, beating until blended.

2. Combine flour and salt; add to butter mixture, beating at low speed until blended. Cover and chill dough 1 hour.

3. Preheat oven to 350°. Shape dough into 1-inch balls. Lightly beat egg whites. Dip each dough ball into egg white; roll in pecans. Place 2 inches apart on ungreased baking sheets. Press thumb in each dough ball to make an indentation.

4. Bake at 350° for 15 minutes. Cool 1 minute on baking sheets, and remove to wire racks to cool completely. Press centers again with thumb while cookies are still warm; fill center of each cookie with jam.

desserts

243

CELEBRATORY

MANGOES

Mangoes were once considered as exotic as the countries where they grew. Their deep golden flesh reminded us of the sunny climates required to ripen them into juicy sweetness. They still bring to mind warm breezes, but mangoes have now become a staple in Southern supermarkets.

Although their peak season runs from May to September, many times they can be found year-round in the produce section, along with jars of mango slices. Jarred slices can often be substituted, but don't be intimidated by fresh mangoes.

A ripe mango should have a faintly sweet aroma and yellow skin blushed with red. To ripen mangoes, keep them at room temperature, or store them in a paper bag. (Don't refrigerate them until they're fully ripe.)

Tex-Mex shrimp cocktail

(pictured at left)

Fiery jalapeño pepper jelly adds a sweet little kick to this traditional dish.

makes: 4 to 6 servings
hands-on time: 15 min.   total time: 4 hr., 15 min.

- ¼ cup hot red jalapeño pepper jelly
- 1 Tbsp. lime zest
- ¼ cup fresh lime juice
- 1 lb. peeled, large cooked shrimp
- 1 cup diced mango
- ½ cup diced red bell pepper
- ¼ cup chopped fresh cilantro
- 1 small avocado, diced

Garnish: lime wedges

1. Whisk together first 3 ingredients. Pour into a large zip-top plastic freezer bag; add shrimp and next 3 ingredients, turning to coat. Seal and chill 4 hours, turning occasionally. Add avocado. Garnish, if desired.

spring salsa

makes: 3½ cups
hands-on time: 15 min.   total time: 15 min.

- 1½ cups cherry tomatoes, seeded and chopped
- 1 cup frozen whole kernel corn, thawed
- ¼ cup chopped red onion
- 2 Tbsp. chopped fresh cilantro
- 1 garlic clove, minced
- 1 jalapeño pepper, seeded and minced
- 2 Tbsp. fresh lime juice

Salt and pepper to taste

Tortilla chips

1. Stir together first 7 ingredients. Season with salt and pepper to taste. Cover and chill until ready to serve (up to 3 hours). Serve with chips.

stuffed mushrooms with pecans

makes: 8 appetizer servings
hands-on time: 28 min.   total time: 53 min.

2   medium leeks
1   (16-oz.) package fresh
     mushrooms (about
     24 medium-size mushrooms)
1   tsp. salt, divided
2   shallots, minced
2   garlic cloves, minced
2   Tbsp. olive oil
½   cup grated Parmesan cheese,
     divided
¼   cup fine, dry breadcrumbs
¼   cup pecans, chopped
2   Tbsp. chopped fresh basil
Garnish: fresh basil sprigs

1. Preheat oven to 350°. Remove and discard root ends and dark green tops of leeks. Thinly slice leeks, and rinse thoroughly under cold running water to remove grit and sand.

2. Rinse mushrooms, and pat dry. Remove and discard stems. Place mushrooms, upside down, on a wire rack in an aluminum foil-lined jelly-roll pan. Sprinkle with ½ tsp. salt; invert mushrooms.

3. Bake at 350° for 15 minutes.

4. Sauté leeks, shallots, and garlic in hot oil in a large skillet over medium heat 3 to 5 minutes or until tender. Transfer mixture to a large bowl. Stir in ¼ cup Parmesan cheese, next 3 ingredients, and remaining ½ tsp. salt until well combined. Spoon 1 heaping teaspoonful leek mixture into each mushroom cap. Sprinkle with remaining ¼ cup Parmesan cheese. Bake at 350° for 10 minutes or until golden. Garnish, if desired.

TASTE OF AUTUMN

MUSHROOMS

Versatile mushrooms have a robust and earthy flavor making them the perfect ingredient in everything from starters to side dishes to tasty sauces. When buying fresh mushrooms, choose those that are smooth and have a dry top. Refrigerate fresh mushrooms, unwashed, for no more than 3 days. They're best kept in a cloth or paper bag that allows them to breathe. Clean fresh mushrooms with a mushroom brush or damp paper towel just before using.

Jordan rolls *(pictured on opposite page)*

makes: 1½ dozen
hands-on time: 25 min.   total time: 1 hr., 35 min.

½ cup sugar
2 (¼-oz.) envelopes rapid-rise
   yeast
1½ tsp. salt
5 cups all-purpose flour, divided
½ cup shortening
2 large eggs, lightly beaten
1½ cups warm water
   (100° to 110°)
¾ cup butter, melted and divided

1. Combine first 3 ingredients and 2 cups flour in a large bowl. Cut in shortening with a fork or pastry blender until crumbly. Stir in eggs. (Mixture will be lumpy and dry.) Stir in warm water, ½ cup melted butter, and remaining 3 cups flour until well blended. (Mixture will remain lumpy.) Cover with a kitchen towel, and let rise in a warm place (85°), free from drafts, 20 minutes. (Rolls will rise only slightly.)

2. Turn dough out onto a floured surface. Sprinkle lightly with flour; knead three to four times. Pat or roll into a 13- x 9-inch rectangle (about ¾ inch thick). Cut dough into 18 rectangles using a pizza cutter. Place in a lightly greased 13- x 9-inch pan, and cover with towel. Let rise in a warm place (85°), free from drafts, 20 minutes.

3. Preheat oven to 350°. Bake rolls 25 minutes. Brush with remaining ¼ cup melted butter, and bake 5 more minutes or until golden.

pimiento cheese rolls

makes: 1 dozen
hands-on time: 15 min.   total time: 1 hr., 15 min.

1 (25-oz.) package frozen
   Southern-style biscuits
All-purpose flour
2 cups pimiento cheese

1. Arrange biscuits, with sides touching, in 3 rows of 4 biscuits on a lightly floured surface. Let stand 30 to 45 minutes or until biscuits are thawed but cool to the touch.

2. Preheat oven to 375°. Sprinkle biscuits lightly with flour. Press edges together, and pat to form a 10- x 12-inch rectangle of dough; spread dough with pimiento cheese.

3. Roll up, starting at one long end; cut into 12 (1-inch-thick) slices. Place 1 slice into each muffin cup of a lightly greased 12-cup muffin pan.

4. Bake at 375° for 20 to 25 minutes or until golden. Cool in pan on a wire rack 5 minutes; remove from pan, and serve immediately.

note: We tested with Pillsbury Grands! Southern Style Biscuits.

Y'ALL ENJOY

Casual Cajun Supper

8 servings

Big Easy Gumbo   Super-Moist Cornbread

Creole Bread Pudding with Bourbon Sauce *(page 217)*

---

super-moist cornbread (pictured on opposite page, top left)

makes: 8 servings   hands-on time: 10 min.   total time: 40 min.

⅓ cup butter
1 (8-oz.) container sour cream
2 large eggs, lightly beaten
1 (8-oz.) can cream-style corn
1 cup self-rising white cornmeal mix

1. Preheat oven to 400°. Heat butter in a 9-inch cast-iron skillet in oven 5 minutes or until butter melts.

2. Combine sour cream, eggs, and corn in a medium bowl. Whisk in cornmeal mix just until combined. Whisk in melted butter. Pour batter into hot skillet. Bake at 400° for 30 minutes or until golden.

big easy gumbo (pictured on opposite page, bottom right)

makes: 8 to 10 servings
hands-on time: 18 min.   total time: 48 min.

½ lb. andouille sausage
½ cup peanut oil
½ cup all-purpose flour
1 cup chopped sweet onion
1 cup chopped green bell pepper
1 cup chopped celery
2 tsp. Creole seasoning
2 tsp. minced garlic
3 (14-oz.) cans chicken broth
4 cups shredded cooked chicken
1½ cups frozen black-eyed peas, thawed
1 lb. peeled, large raw shrimp

1. Cut sausage into ¼-inch-thick slices; set aside. Heat oil in a large Dutch oven over medium-high heat; gradually whisk in flour, and cook, whisking constantly, 5 to 7 minutes or until flour is chocolate colored. (Do not burn mixture.)

2. Reduce heat to medium. Stir in onion and next 4 ingredients, and cook, stirring constantly, 3 minutes. Gradually stir in chicken broth; add chicken, black-eyed peas, and sausage. Increase heat to medium-high, and bring to a boil. Reduce heat to low, and simmer, stirring occasionally, 20 minutes. Add shrimp, and cook 5 minutes or just until shrimp turn pink.

note: We tested with Zatarain's Creole Seasoning and Savoie's Andouille Sausage.

shrimp pesto pizza

makes: 6 servings   hands-on time: 37 min.   total time: 37 min.

Vegetable cooking spray
1   lb. unpeeled, large raw
    shrimp
1   large yellow onion, chopped
1   red bell pepper, chopped
1/4 tsp. salt
1/4 tsp. pepper
1 1/2 tsp. olive oil
1 1/2 lb. bakery pizza dough
All-purpose flour
Plain yellow cornmeal
1/2 cup Garden Pesto*
3/4 cup freshly grated Parmesan
    cheese

1. Coat cold cooking grate of grill with cooking spray, and place on grill. Preheat grill to 300° to 350° (medium) heat. Peel shrimp, and slice in half lengthwise; devein, if desired.

2. Sauté onion, bell pepper, salt, and pepper in 1/2 tsp. hot oil in a large skillet over medium heat 5 minutes or until tender. Transfer onion mixture to a large bowl. Sauté shrimp in remaining 1 tsp. hot oil 3 minutes or just until shrimp turn pink. Add shrimp to onion mixture, and toss.

3. Divide dough into 6 equal portions. Lightly sprinkle flour on a large surface. Roll each portion into a 6-inch round (about 1/4-inch thick). Carefully transfer pizza dough rounds to a cutting board or baking sheet sprinkled with cornmeal.

4. Slide pizza dough rounds onto cooking grate of grill; spread Garden Pesto over rounds, and top with shrimp mixture. Sprinkle each with 2 Tbsp. Parmesan cheese.

5. Grill, covered with grill lid, 4 minutes. Rotate pizzas one-quarter turn, and grill, covered with grill lid, 5 to 6 more minutes or until pizza crusts are cooked. Serve immediately.

*Refrigerated store-bought pesto may be substituted.

garden pesto

makes: 1 1/4 cups   hands-on time: 10 min.   total time: 23 min.

1/4 cup pine nuts
1/4 cup chopped pecans
2 1/2 cups firmly packed fresh basil
    leaves
1/2 cup chopped fresh parsley
2   garlic cloves, chopped
1/3 cup olive oil
3/4 cup (3 oz.) shredded Parmesan
    cheese
1/3 cup olive oil

1. Preheat oven to 350°. Bake pine nuts and pecans in a single layer in a shallow pan 8 minutes or until toasted and fragrant, stirring halfway through. Cool 5 minutes. Process basil leaves, parsley, garlic, and 1/3 cup olive oil in a food processor until a coarse paste forms. Add nuts and Parmesan cheese, and process until blended. With processor running, pour 1/3 cup olive oil through food chute in a slow, steady stream; process until smooth. Cover and chill for up to 5 days.

Y'ALL ENJOY

Birthday Dinner

12 servings

Tiny Tomato Tarts *(page 47)*

Honey Bourbon-Glazed Ham

Scalloped Sweet Potato Stacks *(page 59)*   Simple Grilled Asparagus *(page 106)*

Sweet Green Tomato Corn Muffins *(page 50)*

Mama's German Chocolate Cake *(page 276)*

---

honey bourbon-glazed ham (pictured on opposite page, top left)

makes: 15 servings
hands-on time: 20 min.   total time: 3 hr., 20 min.

1 (9¼-lb.) fully cooked,
   bone-in ham
40 whole cloves
½ cup firmly packed light
   brown sugar
½ cup honey
½ cup bourbon
⅓ cup Creole mustard
⅓ cup molasses

1. Preheat oven to 350°. Remove skin from ham, and trim fat to ¼-inch thickness. Make shallow cuts in fat 1 inch apart in a diamond pattern; insert cloves in centers of diamonds. Place ham in an aluminum foil-lined 13- x 9-inch pan.

2. Stir together brown sugar and next 4 ingredients; spoon over ham.

3. Bake at 350° on lowest oven rack 2 hours and 30 minutes, basting with pan juices every 30 minutes. Shield ham with foil after 1 hour to prevent excessive browning. Remove ham from oven, and let stand 30 minutes.

Try This Twist!

honey-bourbon boneless glazed ham: Substitute 1 (4-lb.) smoked, fully cooked boneless ham for bone-in. Reduce cloves to 3 (do not insert into ham). Stir together brown sugar mixture as directed in Step 2; stir in cloves. Place ham in a foil-lined 13- x 9-inch pan. Pour sauce over ham. Bake as directed, reducing bake time to 1 hour and basting every 30 minutes. makes: 10 servings; hands-on time: 10 min.; total time: 1 hr., 10 min.

apricot-pineapple sweet ribs

makes: 4 to 6 servings
hands-on time: 20 min.   total time: 3 hr., 50 min., including rub, seasoning and glaze

2 slabs baby back ribs
   (about 2 lb. each)
Rib Dry Rub
Rib Liquid Seasoning
Sweet Barbecue Glaze

1. Remove thin membrane from back of each slab by slicing into it, and then pulling it off. (This will make ribs more tender.) Generously apply Rib Dry Rub on both sides of ribs, pressing gently to adhere.

2. Light one side of grill, heating to 250° to 300° (low) heat; leave other side unlit. Place slabs, meat side up, over unlit side, and grill, covered with grill lid, 2 hours and 15 minutes, maintaining temperature inside grill between 225° and 250°.

3. Remove slabs from grill. Place each slab, meat side down, on a large piece of heavy-duty aluminum foil. (Foil should be large enough to completely wrap slab.) Pour ½ cup of Rib Liquid Seasoning over each slab. Tightly wrap each slab in foil. Return slabs to unlit side of grill. Grill, covered with grill lid, 1 hour.

4. Remove slabs; unwrap and discard foil. Brush Sweet Barbecue Glaze on both sides of slabs. Grill slabs, covered with grill lid, on unlit side of grill 15 minutes or until caramelized.

Rib Dry Rub: Stir together ¼ cup firmly packed dark brown sugar, 4 tsp. garlic salt, 4 tsp. chili powder, 2 tsp. salt, 1 tsp. ground black pepper, ½ tsp. celery salt, ¼ tsp. ground white pepper, ¼ tsp. ground red pepper, and ¼ tsp. ground cinnamon. Store in an airtight container for up to 1 month. makes: about ½ cup

Rib Liquid Seasoning: Stir together ½ cup pineapple juice, ½ cup apricot nectar, 1 Tbsp. Rib Dry Rub, 1½ tsp. balsamic vinegar, and 1½ tsp. minced garlic. Store in an airtight container in refrigerator for up to 2 weeks. makes: about 1 cup

Sweet Barbecue Glaze: Stir together 1¼ cups premium tomato-based barbecue sauce and ¼ cup honey. Store in an airtight container in refrigerator up for to 2 weeks. makes: about 1½ cups

special occasions

259

chicken marsala

makes: 4 servings
hands-on time: 40 min.   total time: 45 min.

3   Tbsp. butter, divided
1   cup pecan pieces, divided
⅓   cup all-purpose flour
4   skinned and boned chicken
     breasts (about 1½ lb.)
1   tsp. salt
½   tsp. pepper
2   Tbsp. olive oil
8   oz. assorted mushrooms,
     trimmed and sliced
2   shallots, sliced
¾   cup chicken broth
½   cup Marsala
¼   cup coarsely chopped fresh
     flat-leaf parsley

1. Melt 1 Tbsp. butter in a small nonstick skillet over medium-low heat; add ⅔ cup pecans, and cook, stirring often, 4 to 5 minutes or until toasted and fragrant.

2. Process flour and remaining ⅓ cup pecans in a food processor until finely ground; place flour mixture in a large shallow bowl.

3. Place chicken between 2 sheets of heavy-duty plastic wrap; flatten to ¼-inch thickness, using a rolling pin or flat side of a meat mallet. Sprinkle chicken with salt and pepper; lightly dredge in flour mixture.

4. Melt remaining 2 Tbsp. butter with olive oil in a large nonstick skillet over medium-high heat; add chicken, and cook 2 to 3 minutes on each side or until golden brown and desired degree of doneness. Remove chicken from skillet.

5. Add mushrooms and shallots to skillet; sauté 3 minutes or until mushrooms are tender. Add broth and Marsala to skillet, stirring to loosen particles from bottom of skillet. Bring mixture to a boil, reduce heat to medium, and cook, stirring occasionally, 5 minutes or until sauce is slightly thickened. Return chicken to skillet, and cook 1 to 2 minutes or until thoroughly heated.

6. Transfer chicken to a serving platter; spoon mushroom-Marsala mixture over chicken, and sprinkle with parsley and toasted pecans.

celebratory

Y'ALL ENJOY

Tex-Mex Fiesta

6 to 8 servings

Chicken Enchiladas

Three Sisters Salad *(page 269)*

Mango Tango *(page 265)*

Mexican Chocolate Ice-Cream Pie *(page 270)*

---

chicken enchiladas (pictured on opposite page, top left)

makes: 6 to 8 servings
hands-on time: 25 min.
total time: 2 hr., 45 min., including salsa

1   cup diced sweet onion
3   garlic cloves, minced
1   Tbsp. canola oil
2   cups chopped fresh baby spinach
2   (4.5-oz.) cans chopped green chiles, drained
3   cups shredded cooked chicken
1   (8-oz.) package ⅓-less-fat cream cheese, cubed and softened
2   cups (8 oz.) shredded pepper Jack cheese
⅓   cup chopped fresh cilantro
Salt and pepper to taste
8   (8-inch) soft taco-size flour tortillas
Vegetable cooking spray
Tomatillo Salsa

1. Preheat oven to 350°. Sauté onion and garlic in hot oil in a large skillet over medium heat 5 minutes or until tender. Add spinach and green chiles; sauté 1 to 2 minutes or until spinach is wilted. Stir in chicken and next 3 ingredients, and cook, stirring constantly, 5 minutes or until cheeses melt. Add salt and pepper to taste. Spoon about ¾ cup chicken mixture down center of each tortilla; roll up tortillas.

2. Place rolled tortillas, seam side down, in a lightly greased 13- x 9-inch baking dish. Lightly coat tortillas with cooking spray.

3. Bake at 350° for 30 to 35 minutes or until golden brown. Top with Tomatillo Salsa.

Tomatillo Salsa: Stir together 2 cups diced tomatillo; ⅓ cup sliced green onions; ⅓ cup lightly packed fresh cilantro leaves; 1 jalapeño pepper, seeded and minced; 1 Tbsp. fresh lime juice; and ½ tsp. salt. Cover and chill 1 to 4 hours. Let stand at room temperature 30 minutes. Stir in 1 cup diced avocado just before serving. makes: 3 cups

refried black beans (pictured on opposite page)

Bacon adds a wonderful smokiness to the beans, but you can make this a vegetarian dish by omitting the bacon and substituting 2 Tbsp. oil for the drippings.

makes: 6 servings
hands-on time: 13 min.   total time: 27 min.

4   bacon slices
1   large onion, chopped
2   garlic cloves, minced
1   tsp. ground cumin
½   tsp. ground chipotle chili pepper
¼   tsp. salt
2 (15-oz) cans black beans, drained
6   Tbsp. fresh jalapeño pepper
      slices
¼   cup loosely packed fresh
      cilantro leaves
6   Tbsp. crumbled queso fresco
      (fresh Mexican cheese)
6   lime wedges

1. Cook bacon in a large nonstick skillet over medium-high heat 4 to 5 minutes or until crisp; remove bacon, and drain on paper towels, reserving 2 Tbsp. drippings in skillet. Crumble bacon.

2. Sauté onion, garlic, cumin, chili pepper, and salt in hot drippings over medium heat 5 minutes or until tender. Add beans to skillet. Mash beans over medium heat, and cook 5 to 10 minutes or to desired consistency, adding ¼ cup water, if necessary. Remove from heat; sprinkle with bacon, jalapeño pepper slices, cilantro, and cheese. Serve with lime wedges.

mango tango (pictured on page 263, bottom right)

makes: 6 to 8 servings
hands-on time: 20 min.   total time: 2 hr., 20 min.

¼   cup fresh lime juice
3   Tbsp. sugar
1   Tbsp. seeded and minced
      jalapeño pepper
2   mangoes, peeled and sliced
3   large peaches, peeled and
      sliced
3   cups sliced assorted plums
1   Tbsp. chopped fresh mint
1   Tbsp. chopped fresh cilantro

1. Stir together first 3 ingredients in a large bowl until sugar dissolves. Add mangoes and remaining 4 ingredients, tossing to coat. Cover and chill 2 to 6 hours.

blueberry-gorgonzola salad

makes: 4 servings   (pictured at right, back)
hands-on time: 15 min.   total time: 15 min.

1 (5-oz.) package mixed salad greens	¾ cup sliced fresh chives (about 1-inch pieces)
2 cups fresh blueberries	¾ cup crumbled Gorgonzola cheese
1 cup loosely packed fresh flat-leaf parsley leaves	¾ cup bottled raspberry-walnut vinaigrette
1 cup loosely packed basil leaves	½ cup loosely packed fresh tarragon leaves
1 cup roasted, salted almonds*	

1. Toss together all ingredients in a large serving bowl.

* Glazed walnuts may be substituted.

strawberry-cantaloupe salad

makes: 6 servings   (pictured at right, front)
hands-on time: 18 min.   total time: 18 min.

⅓ cup honey	1 qt. fresh strawberries, quartered
¼ cup fresh lime juice	2 cups cubed cantaloupe
1 tsp. Dijon mustard	⅓ cup torn fresh mint
¼ tsp. salt	½ cup honey-roasted flavored sliced almonds
⅛ tsp. ground red pepper	
¼ cup canola oil	

1. Whisk together first 5 ingredients in a medium bowl. Add oil in a slow, steady stream, whisking constantly until smooth.

2. Toss strawberries, cantaloupe, and mint with ½ cup vinaigrette in a large bowl. Sprinkle with almonds.

BLUEBERRIES

It's hard to imagine a fourth of July get-together without a tasty fruit salad or luscious dessert boasting the flavor of fresh, ripe blueberries. Of all the popular summer fruits, blueberries have an advantage nutritionally speaking. They've earned the distinction as one of the most potent sources of antioxidants. To pick the best of the crop, look for powdery-blue blueberries that are firm and uniform in size. Store them in a single layer, if possible, in a moisture-proof container for up to 5 days, and don't rinse them until you're ready to use them.

three sisters salad (pictured on opposite page)

makes: 8 to 10 servings
hands-on time: 20 min.   total time: 3 hr., 20 min.

2   lb. butternut squash
2   Tbsp. olive oil
1   (15.5-oz.) can cannellini beans,
     drained and rinsed
2   cups fresh corn kernels
½   small red onion, sliced
½   cup chopped fresh basil
Balsamic Vinaigrette
3   cups loosely packed arugula

1. Preheat oven to 400°. Peel and seed butternut squash; cut into ¾-inch cubes. Toss squash with olive oil to coat; place in a single layer in a lightly greased aluminum foil-lined 15- x 10-inch jelly-roll pan. Bake at 400° for 20 minutes or until squash is just tender and begins to brown (do not overcook), stirring once after 10 minutes. Cool completely (about 20 minutes) Toss together cannellini beans, next 4 ingredients, and squash; cover and chill 2 to 4 hours. Toss with arugula just before serving.

Balsamic Vinaigrette: Whisk together 2 Tbsp. balsamic vinegar; 1 large shallot, minced; 1 tsp. minced garlic; ½ Tbsp. light brown sugar; ¼ tsp. salt; and ¼ tsp. seasoned pepper. Gradually add ¼ cup canola oil in a slow, steady stream, whisking until blended.

green beans with roasted tomatoes

makes: 6 servings
hands-on time: 32 min.   total time: 1 hr., 12 min.

8   plum tomatoes (about 1½ lbs.),
     halved lengthwise
3   large shallots, halved lengthwise
3   large garlic cloves, sliced
1   Tbsp. brown sugar
1   tsp. kosher salt
½   tsp. freshly ground pepper
1   Tbsp. olive oil
1   lb. fresh green beans, trimmed
2   tsp. olive oil
½   tsp. kosher salt
2   Tbsp. white balsamic vinegar
2   Tbsp. chopped mixed fresh
     herbs

1. Preheat oven to 450°. Arrange tomatoes, cut side up, in a single layer in a 15- x 10-inch jelly-roll pan. Place shallots and garlic around tomatoes. Sprinkle brown sugar, 1 tsp. salt, and pepper evenly over vegetables; drizzle with 1 Tbsp. oil. Bake at 450° for 30 minutes or until tomatoes begin to caramelize. Cool in pan 10 minutes.

2. Meanwhile, cook green beans in boiling salted water to cover 4 minutes or just until tender. Drain well. Sauté green beans in 2 tsp. hot oil in a large skillet over medium-high heat 3 minutes or until lightly browned. Remove from heat; sprinkle with ½ tsp. salt.

3. Spoon tomato mixture and pan juices into a large bowl; coarsely chop tomatoes and shallots, using kitchen shears. Add balsamic vinegar and herbs to tomato mixture; toss well. Arrange green beans on a serving platter; spoon tomato mixture over green beans.

Mexican chocolate ice-cream pie

A crisp, over-the-rim graham cracker crust spiked with ground cinnamon and red pepper adds a spicy cowboy kick to this showstopping pie. Make and freeze it up to one month ahead.

makes: 8 servings
hands-on time: 30 min.   total time: 10 hr., 50 min.

3   cups cinnamon graham cracker crumbs (about 22 whole crackers), divided
1/2 cup butter, melted
1/4 tsp. ground red pepper
1   (4-oz.) semisweet chocolate baking bar, finely chopped
1   (3.5-oz.) package roasted glazed pecan pieces
1   pt. chocolate ice cream, softened
1   pt. coffee ice cream, softened
1   cup whipping cream
1/4 cup coffee liqueur
Garnish: coarsely chopped chocolate

1. Preheat oven to 350°. Stir together 2½ cups cinnamon graham cracker crumbs and next 2 ingredients; firmly press mixture on bottom and up sides of a lightly greased 9-inch pie plate. Bake 10 to 12 minutes or until lightly browned. Cool completely on a wire rack (about 30 minutes).

2. Stir together semisweet chocolate, pecan pieces, and remaining ½ cup cinnamon graham cracker crumbs. Reserve ½ cup chocolate-pecan mixture to top pie.

3. Spread chocolate ice cream in bottom of prepared crust; top with remaining chocolate-pecan mixture. Freeze 30 minutes. Spread coffee ice cream over chocolate mixture. Cover and freeze 8 hours.

4. Beat whipping cream and coffee liqueur at medium speed with an electric mixer until stiff peaks form. Spread whipped cream mixture over pie; sprinkle with reserved ½ cup chocolate-pecan mixture. Cover and freeze 1 hour or until whipped cream is firm. Let stand 10 to 15 minutes before serving. Garnish, if desired.

Valentine's cookies (lemon butter cookies)

makes: about 4 dozen (2¼-inch) or 1½ dozen (4-inch) cookies
hands-on time: 30 min.
total time: 1 hr., 29 min., including glaze

1 cup butter, softened
1 tsp. lemon zest
1 cup powdered sugar
2 cups all-purpose flour
¼ tsp. salt
Parchment paper
Colorful Glaze
Coarse sugar sprinkles

1. Preheat oven to 325°. Beat butter and zest at medium speed with a heavy-duty electric stand mixer until creamy. Gradually add powdered sugar, beating well.

2. Combine flour and salt; gradually add to butter mixture, beating until blended. Shape dough into a disc.

3. Roll dough to ⅛-inch thickness on a lightly floured surface. Cut with a 2¼- or 3¼-inch heart-shaped cutter; place ½ inch apart on parchment paper-lined baking sheets. If desired, cut 1 or 2 holes at top of each cookie (to hang or thread ribbon through after baking).

4. Bake at 325° for 12 to 14 minutes or until edges are lightly browned. Cool on baking sheets 5 minutes. Transfer to wire racks; cool completely (about 20 minutes). Spread Colorful Glaze on top of cookies. Sprinkle with sugar, if desired.

colorful glaze

makes: about 1 cup   hands-on time: 5 min.   total time: 5 min.

1 (16-oz.) package powdered sugar
Food coloring paste

1. Stir together powdered sugar and 6 Tbsp. water. Tint glaze with desired amount of food coloring paste, and stir until blended.

note: Purchase food coloring paste at cake-supply and crafts stores or supercenters.

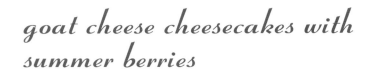

goat cheese cheesecakes with summer berries

makes: 10 servings
hands-on time: 30 min.
total time: 8 hr., 27 min., including berries

1   cup graham cracker crumbs
4   Tbsp. melted butter
1   Tbsp. sugar
Pinch of salt
1   (0.25-oz.) envelope unflavored
     gelatin
⅓   cup milk
½   (8-oz.) package cream cheese,
     softened
1   (4-oz.) goat cheese log
⅓   cup sugar
2   tsp. lemon zest
Pinch of salt
1¼ cups heavy cream
Summer Berries
Garnish: lemon zest

1. Stir together graham cracker crumbs, butter, sugar, and salt. Divide mixture among 10 (8-oz.) glasses (about 1 heaping table-spoonful each); press down mixture. Chill 30 minutes.

2. Sprinkle gelatin over milk in a small saucepan, and let stand 1 min-ute. Cook milk mixture over medium-low heat, whisking constantly, 3 to 5 minutes or until gelatin is dissolved. Remove from heat.

3. Beat cream cheese and goat cheese at medium speed with a heavy-duty electric stand mixer, using whisk attachment, until smooth. Beat in ⅓ cup sugar, lemon zest, and salt. Slowly add milk mixture, beating until combined.

4. Beat heavy cream at high speed, using whisk attachment, until soft peaks form. Gently fold into cheese mixture. Divide mixture among glasses (about ⅓ cup each). Cover and chill 6 to 48 hours. Let stand at room temperature 30 minutes. Top with Summer Berries just before serving. Garnish, if desired.

summer berries

makes: about 3 cups
hands-on time: 5 min.   total time: 1 hr., 5 min.

1   cup fresh blackberries
1   cup fresh blueberries
1   cup fresh raspberries
½   cup sugar
2 Tbsp. fresh lemon juice

1. Stir together all ingredients; cover and chill 1 hour.

Mama's German chocolate cake

(pictured on page 257)

makes: 12 servings
hands-on time: 30 min.   total time: 3 hr., 48 min.

Parchment paper
2   (4-oz.) packages sweet
     chocolate baking bars
2   cups all-purpose flour
1   tsp. baking soda
¼   tsp. salt
1   cup butter, softened
2   cups sugar
4   large eggs
1   tsp. vanilla extract
1   cup buttermilk
Coconut-Pecan Frosting
Garnish: chocolate-dipped toasted
     pecan halves

1. Preheat oven to 350°. Lightly grease 3 (9-inch) round cake pans; line bottoms with parchment paper, and lightly grease paper.

2. Microwave chocolate baking bars and ½ cup water in a large microwave-safe bowl at HIGH for 1 to 1½ minutes or until chocolate is melted and smooth, stirring once halfway through.

3. Combine flour and next 2 ingredients in a medium bowl.

4. Beat butter and sugar at medium speed with an electric mixer until fluffy. Add eggs, 1 at a time, beating just until blended after each addition. Stir in chocolate mixture and vanilla. Add flour mixture alternately with buttermilk, beginning and ending with flour mixture. Beat at low speed just until blended after each addition.

5. Pour batter into prepared pans.

6. Bake at 350° for 25 to 30 minutes or until a wooden pick inserted in center comes out clean. Remove from oven, and gently run a knife around outer edge of cake layers to loosen from sides of pans. Cool in pans on wire racks 15 minutes. Remove from pans to wire racks; discard parchment paper. Cool completely (about 1 hour). Spread Coconut-Pecan Frosting between layers and on top and sides of cake. Garnish, if desired.

note: We tested with Baker's German's Sweet Chocolate Bar.

coconut-pecan frosting

makes: about 5 cups
hands-on time: 25 min.   total time: 1 hr., 38 min.

2   cups chopped pecans
1   (12-oz.) can evaporated milk
1½ cups sugar
¾   cup butter
6   egg yolks, lightly beaten
2   cups sweetened flaked
     coconut
1½ teaspoons vanilla extract

1. Preheat oven to 350°. Bake pecans 8 to 10 minutes or until toasted and fragrant, stirring halfway through. Cool completely (about 20 minutes). Meanwhile, cook evaporated milk, sugar, butter, and egg yolks in a heavy 3-qt. saucepan over medium heat, stirring constantly, 3 to 4 minutes or until butter melts and sugar dissolves. Cook, stirring constantly, 12 to 14 minutes or until mixture becomes a light caramel color, bubbles, and reaches a pudding-like thickness.

2. Remove pan from heat; stir in coconut, vanilla, and pecans. Transfer mixture to a bowl. Let stand, stirring occasionally, 45 minutes or until cooled and spreading consistency.

SIT A SPELL
Nuts In the South

Southerners associate pecans with two great pleasures—food and shade. During the summertime, "Let's sit out here under the pecan trees" is an invitation to pull your lawn chair under a leafy canopy and sip a glass of sweet tea.

Gathering the bounty from these trees is a race between man and squirrel. Sometimes the squirrel wins, but it's hard to begrudge any living creature that delightful flavor. Shelling pecans is a labor of love. We do it willingly, with visions of Thanksgiving dancing in our heads. We're dreaming of pecan pie and sweet potato casserole topped with that magical mixture of brown sugar, butter, and pecans. Some cooks even upgrade their brittle from peanut to pecan. (That's considered a little uppity in some circles.)

Butter-pecan anything will make you pick up the phone and call your mama to tell her all about it. If you don't believe that, have a scoop of homemade butter-pecan ice cream and try not to shout about how good it was. I think that's the real reason we love all our favorite foods— they bring us together and give us something to talk about. So I guess that makes not two, but three great pleasures we take from pecans: food, shade, and good conversation.

VFL

strawberry birthday cake

makes: 16 servings
hands-on time: 53 min.   total time: 2 hr., 46 min.

Cake Layers:

1   cup butter, softened
2   cups granulated sugar
3   large eggs
2¾ cups all-purpose soft-wheat
    flour
2   tsp. baking powder
½   tsp. salt
1   cup milk
1   vanilla bean

Strawberry Compote:

1   vanilla bean
1½ cups chopped strawberries
½   cup granulated sugar
1   Tbsp. dark rum

Cream Cheese Frosting:

1½ cups butter, softened
½   (8-oz.) package cream cheese,
    softened
5   cups powdered sugar
2   tsp. vanilla extract
½   tsp. almond extract

Garnish: fresh strawberry halves

1. Prepare Cake Layers: Preheat oven to 350°. Beat butter at medium speed with an electric mixer until creamy; gradually add sugar, beating well. Add eggs, 1 at a time, beating until blended after each addition.

2. Combine flour, baking powder, and salt; add to butter mixture alternately with milk, beginning and ending with flour mixture. Beat at low speed until blended after each addition, stopping to scrape bowl as needed. Split vanilla bean lengthwise, and scrape out seeds. Stir seeds into batter; reserve bean for another use. Pour batter into 2 greased and floured 8-inch round cake pans with 2-inch sides.

3. Bake at 350° for 30 to 34 minutes or until a wooden pick inserted in center comes out clean. Cool in pans on wire racks 10 minutes; remove from pans to wire racks, and cool completely (about 1 hour).

4. Prepare Compote: Split vanilla bean lengthwise, and scrape out seeds. Stir together vanilla bean and seeds, strawberries, and sugar in a medium saucepan. Cook over medium heat, stirring occasionally, 10 minutes or until strawberries are soft and mixture is slightly syrupy. Remove from heat; discard vanilla bean. Stir in rum. Cool completely (about 30 min).

5. Prepare Frosting: Beat butter and cream cheese at medium speed with an electric mixer about 3 minutes or until creamy. Gradually add powdered sugar, beating at low speed until smooth. Beat at medium speed 1 minute or until fluffy. Stir in extracts. Garnish, if desired.

6. Using a serrated knife, slice cake layers in half horizontally to make 4 layers. Place 1 layer, cut side up, on a cake plate. Spread with half of Strawberry Compote. Top with another cake layer; spread with about ¾ cup Cream Cheese Frosting. Place another cake layer on top of frosting; spread with remaining Strawberry Compote. Top with remaining cake layer. Spread 1½ cups frosting on top and sides of cake to create a thin coat of frosting. Chill cake 30 minutes. Spread top and sides of cake with remaining Cream Cheese Frosting. Store in refrigerator.

special occasions

key lime pie ice cream

makes: about 1 qt.
hands-on time: 20 min.   total time: 9 hr., 20 min.

½ cup granular sweetener
   for ice cream*
2 Tbsp. cornstarch
⅛ tsp. salt
2 cups 2% reduced-fat
   milk
1 cup half-and-half

1 egg yolk
1 tsp. Key lime zest
⅓ cup Key lime juice
½ cup coarsely crushed
   graham crackers
Garnish: lime zest

1. Whisk together first 3 ingredients in a large heavy saucepan. Gradually whisk in milk and half-and-half. Cook over medium heat, stirring constantly, 8 to 10 minutes or until mixture thickens slightly. Remove from heat.

2. Whisk egg yolk until slightly thickened. Gradually whisk about 1 cup hot cream mixture into yolk. Add yolk mixture to remaining hot cream mixture, whisking constantly.

3. Pour mixture through a fine wire-mesh strainer into a bowl, discarding solids. Cool 1 hour, stirring occasionally. Place plastic wrap directly on cream mixture; chill 8 to 24 hours.

4. Pour mixture into freezer container of a 1½-qt. electric ice-cream maker, and freeze according to manufacturer's instructions; stir in Key lime zest, Key lime juice, and crushed graham crackers halfway through freezing. Let stand at room temperature 5 to 10 minutes before serving. Garnish, if desired.

*Granulated sugar may be substituted.

Taste of Summertime

Hand-cranked ice cream has divine associations for me—and I'm not just talking about the flavor. When I was a child, our small-town church would have revival services every summer. A "vis'tin' preacher" would take charge of the pulpit, and guest soloists who could really hit those high notes would wow us with special arrangements of "How Great Thou Art" and "Amazing Grace." The congregational singing would just about raise the roof off the church. (And the sermons were long enough to make even the most God-fearing children squirm in our pews, forcing our mothers to give us The Look.)

For a whole week before the revival, we'd hold nightly cottage prayer meetings in church members' homes, with refreshments following. Homemade ice cream was a staple at those gatherings. I can remember watching the adults in our family take turns cranking the ice cream on my grandmother's porch, preparing to serve the congregation once the sun went down and the house cooled off. (Central air was a distant dream back then.) Rock salt would tumble and twirl as the crank went round and round. And once we had said the last "Amen" and the lid came off that icy metal canister, a houseful of happy Baptists would line up to be served what can only be described as a heavenly taste of summertime.

VFL

SITA SPELL

derby julep

makes: 1 serving
hands-on time: 5 min.   total time: 5 min., not including syrup

3   to 5 fresh mint leaves
2   Tbsp. desired julep syrup
     (see right)
Crushed ice
¼   cup bourbon
1   fresh mint sprig

1. Place mint leaves and syrup in a chilled julep cup, and muddle. Pack cup tightly with crushed ice; add bourbon and mint sprig.

julep syrups

Set up a mint julep bar with an assortment of flavored syrups at your next gathering.

mint syrup: Boil 1 ½ cups sugar and 1 ½ cups water, stirring often, 2 to 3 minutes or until sugar dissolves. Remove from heat; add 15 fresh mint sprigs, and cool completely. Cover and chill 24 hours. Strain syrup; discard solids.

grapefruit-honey syrup: Prepare Mint Syrup as directed, reducing sugar to ½ cup and stirring ¾ cup fresh grapefruit juice, ½ cup honey, 3 (2- x 4-inch) grapefruit rind strips, and rind from 1 lime, cut into strips, into sugar mixture with mint. For julep, muddle with 1 small grapefruit rind strip.

peach-basil syrup: Prepare Mint Syrup as directed, substituting basil for mint and stirring 2 (5.5-oz.) cans peach nectar and 1 split vanilla bean into sugar mixture with basil. For julep, muddle with 1 peach slice.

blackberry syrup: Prepare Mint Syrup as directed, adding 6 oz. fresh blackberries, halved, with mint. For julep, muddle with 2 fresh blackberries.

pineapple-lemongrass syrup: Prepare Mint Syrup as directed, reducing granulated sugar to 1 cup, adding ½ cup light brown sugar to granulated sugar and water, and stirring 1 cup pineapple juice, 2 Tbsp. fresh lime juice, and 3 (3-inch) pieces fresh lemongrass into sugar mixture with mint after removing from heat. For julep, muddle with 1 small fresh pineapple chunk.

METRIC EQUIVALENTS

The recipes that appear in this cookbook use the standard U.S. method for measuring liquid and dry or solid ingredients (teaspoons, tablespoons, and cups). The information on this chart is provided to help cooks outside the United States successfully use these recipes. All equivalents are approximate.

Metric Equivalents for Different Types of Ingredients

A standard cup measure of a dry or solid ingredient will vary in weight depending on the type of ingredient. A standard cup of liquid is the same volume for any type of liquid. Use the following chart when converting standard cup measures to grams (weight) or milliliters (volume).

Standard Cup	Fine Powder (ex. flour)	Grain (ex. rice)	Granular (ex. sugar)	Liquid Solids (ex. butter)	Liquid (ex. milk)
1	140 g	150 g	190 g	200 g	240 ml
¾	105 g	113 g	143 g	150 g	180 ml
⅔	93 g	100 g	125 g	133 g	160 ml
½	70 g	75 g	95 g	100 g	120 ml
⅓	47 g	50 g	63 g	67 g	80 ml
¼	35 g	38 g	48 g	50 g	60 ml
⅛	18 g	19 g	24 g	25 g	30 ml

Useful Equivalents for Dry Ingredients by Weight

(To convert ounces to grams, multiply the number of ounces by 30.)

1 oz	=	1/16 lb	=	30 g
4 oz	=	¼ lb	=	120 g
8 oz	=	½ lb	=	240 g
12 oz	=	¾ lb	=	360 g
16 oz	=	1 lb	=	480 g

Useful Equivalents for Length

(To convert inches to centimeters, multiply the number of inches by 2.5.)

1 in					=	2.5 cm	
6 in	=	½ ft			=	15 cm	
12 in	=	1 ft			=	30 cm	
36 in	=	3 ft	=	1 yd	=	90 cm	
40 in					=	100 cm	= 1 m

Useful Equivalents for Liquid Ingredients by Volume

¼ tsp					=	1 ml	
½ tsp					=	2 ml	
1 tsp					=	5 ml	
3 tsp	=	1 Tbsp		=	½ fl oz	=	15 ml
		2 Tbsp	=	⅛ cup	=	1 fl oz	= 30 ml
		4 Tbsp	=	¼ cup	=	2 fl oz	= 60 ml
		5⅓ Tbsp	=	⅓ cup	=	3 fl oz	= 80 ml
		8 Tbsp	=	½ cup	=	4 fl oz	= 120 ml
		10⅔ Tbsp	=	⅔ cup	=	5 fl oz	= 160 ml
		12 Tbsp	=	¾ cup	=	6 fl oz	= 180 ml
		16 Tbsp	=	1 cup	=	8 fl oz	= 240 ml
	1 pt	=	2 cups	=	16 fl oz	=	480 ml
	1 qt	=	4 cups	=	32 fl oz	=	960 ml
					33 fl oz	=	1000 ml = 1 l

Useful Equivalents for Cooking/Oven Temperatures

	Fahrenheit	Celsius	Gas Mark
Freeze water	32° F	0° C	
Room temperature	68° F	20° C	
Boil water	212° F	100° C	
Bake	325° F	160° C	3
	350° F	180° C	4
	375° F	190° C	5
	400° F	200° C	6
	425° F	220° C	7
	450° F	230° C	8
Broil			Grill

INDEX

index